Contents

GRADE 6

D1299229

Calculate. Do not use a calculator.

①
$$3.9.1$$
$$4.\cancel{0}3$$
$$- \quad 2.98$$
$$1.05$$

②
$$^{1}1806$$
$$3904$$
$$+ \quad 4090$$
$$9800$$

③
$$^{2}5.^{1}43$$
$$\times \quad 6$$
$$32.58$$

④
$$^{1}{}^{6}59$$
$$\times \quad 27$$
$$413$$
$$+118X$$
$$1593$$

⑤
$$\quad\quad 820$$
$$9\overline{)7380}$$
$$-72\downarrow$$
$$\overline{018}\downarrow$$
$$-018\downarrow$$
$$\overline{00.0}$$

⑥
$$\quad\quad 06.48$$
$$5\overline{)32.4}$$
$$-30\downarrow$$
$$\overline{02.4}$$
$$-20$$
$$\overline{040}$$
$$-40$$
$$\overline{00}$$

Find the answers mentally.

⑦ 30 900 ÷ 300 = _____

⑧ 50 x 59 x 2 = _____

⑨ 4 x 12 x 25 = _____

⑩ 61.2 ÷ 6 = _____

⑪ 0.01 x 100 = _____

⑫ 801 ÷ 100 = _____

Use multiplication and addition to check each of the following answers. Put a check mark ✗ in the circle if the answer is correct.

✗ ⑬ 2955 ÷ 5 = 591 ✓ **Check** 2955 ÷ 5 = 591

✗ ⑭ 3939 ÷ 7 = 564 ◯ **Check** 3948 ÷ 7 = 564

✗ ⑮ 2390 ÷ 6 = 398...2 ◯ **Check** _____

Estimate each answer by rounding the number to the nearest ten or thousand. Put a check mark ✔ in the circle if the answer is reasonable.

⑯ 49 x 79 = 4081 ◯ **Estimate** _____

⑰ 3576 ÷ 8 = 447 ◯ **Estimate** _____

⑱ 52 x 41 = 213 ◯ **Estimate** _____

Complete the charts below.

⑲

Decimal	0.7	a.	b.	0.5	0.08	1.13
Fraction with 10 or 100 as denominator	$\frac{7}{10}$	$\frac{29}{100}$	$1\frac{35}{100}$	c.	d.	e.

⑳

Mixed number	$1\frac{1}{2}$	a.	b.	$1\frac{1}{4}$	$4\frac{2}{5}$	$3\frac{7}{8}$
Improper fraction	$\frac{3}{2}$	$\frac{7}{3}$	$\frac{31}{7}$	c.	d.	e.

Fill in the next 3 terms for each of the following patterns.

㉑ 1, 2, 4, 7, 11, _____ , _____ , _____

㉒ 2, 4, 8, 16, 32, _____ , _____ , _____

㉓ 3, 4, 6, 7, 9, _____ , _____ , _____

㉔ 100, 95, 85, 80, 70, _____ , _____ , _____

Calculate the area (A) and perimeter (P) of each of the following shapes.

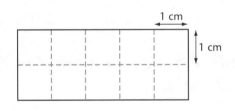

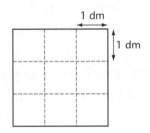

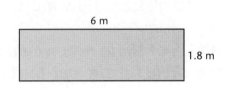

㉕ A = _____ cm²

P = _____ cm

㉖ A = _____ dm²

P = _____ dm

㉗ A = _____ m²

P = _____ m

If Box A is 400 g, determine the mass of the other boxes and answer the question.

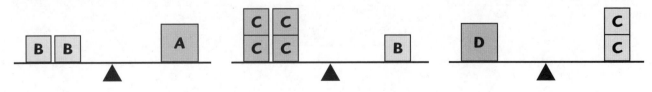

㉘ B = _____ g

㉙ C = _____ g

㉚ D = _____ g

㉛ How many D boxes would make up a mass of 1 kg ? _____

Answer the questions.

㉜ On Sports Day, 300 cans of coke were bought at $0.35 each. How much did they cost in all? $ _____

㉝ 20 boxes of biscuits were purchased at $2.75 per box. How much did they cost in all? $ _____

㉞ 15 boxes of biscuits purchased were eaten. What fraction of the biscuits purchased were left over? _____

㉟ The students were divided into 36 equal teams of 9. How many students were there in all? _____ students

㊱ Give 4 other possible ways to divide all the students into equal groups. Use a calculator if necessary.

_____ groups of _____ students; _____ groups of _____ students;

_____ groups of _____ students; _____ groups of _____ students

㊲ A jug holds 1.5 L of water. The water is poured equally into 10 glasses. How much water is in each glass? _____ mL

Which of these nets would form a prism or a pyramid? Put a check mark ✔ in the circle for the net that could form a prism or a pyramid.

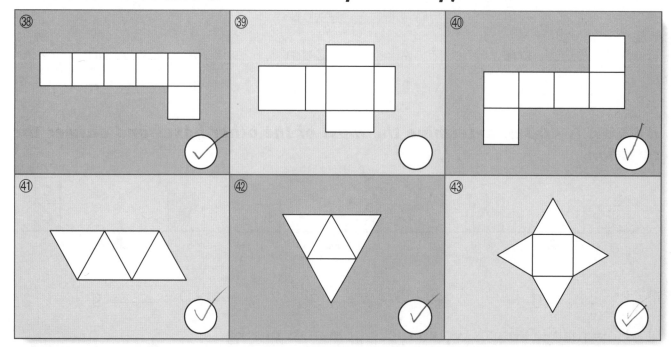

Write the coordinates of the points on the grid and complete the sentence.

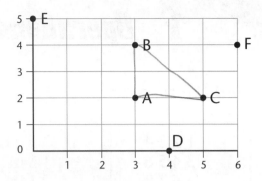

㊹ A (**2** , **3**)　　B (**3** , **4**)

C (**2** , **5**)　　D (**0** , **4**)

E (**0** , **5**)　　F (**4** , **6**)

㊺ The shape formed by joining A , B and C with straight lines is a **triangle** .

Put a check mark ✔ in the circle if the shape can form a tiling pattern.

㊻

Ⓐ　　Ⓑ　　Ⓒ　　Ⓓ　　Ⓔ

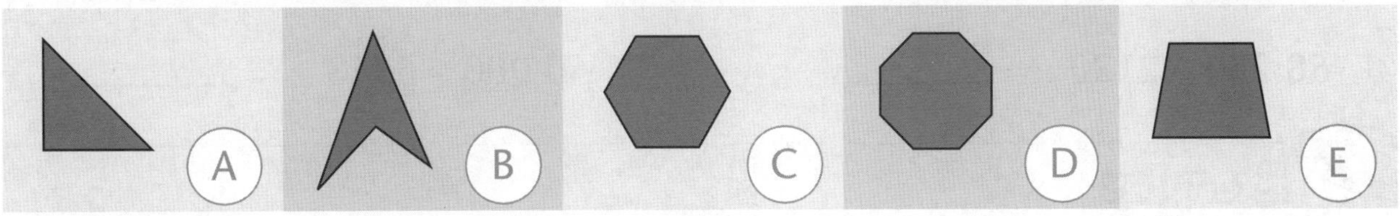

Draw the transformed images.

㊼ Rotate the triangle $\frac{1}{2}$ turn.

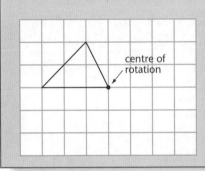

centre of rotation

㊽ Translate the triangle 4 units right and 1 unit down.

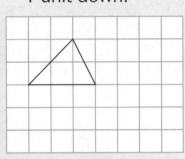

㊾ Reflect the triangle in the line given.

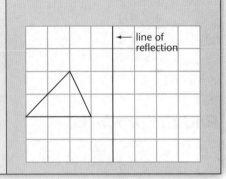

← line of reflection

Look at the tiling pattern. Describe each of the following transformations. Write reflection, rotation or translation.

㊿ B → C　＿＿＿＿＿＿

(51) A → D　＿＿＿＿＿＿

(52) C → F　＿＿＿＿＿＿

(53) A → E　＿＿＿＿＿＿

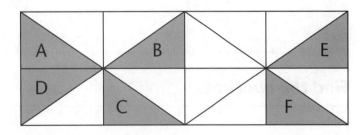

Find the volume of the stone and the apple.

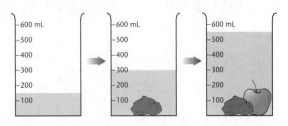

(54) Volume of the stone ＿＿＿＿＿ cm^3

(55) Volume of the apple ＿＿＿＿＿ cm^3

5

1 Operations with Whole Numbers

Find the sums or differences.

①
```
       2
    1234
    3456
    5678
  +  789
  ───────
       7
```

②
```
    3926
    1503
    2198
  +  492
  ───────
```

③
```
    8006
     123
     899
  +    7
  ───────
```

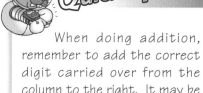

Quick Tip

When doing addition, remember to add the correct digit carried over from the column to the right. It may be greater than 1 for addition with more than 2 addends.

④ 58 239 – 2120 = _____

⑤ 50 000 – 6348 = _____

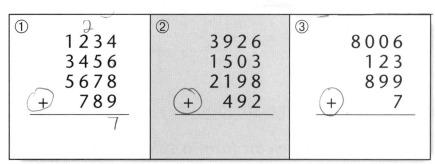

Examples

① a 3-digit number x a 2-digit number

```
     239
   x  28
   ──────
    1912
    4780
   ──────
    6692
```

Steps:
- Multiply the ones.
- Multiply the tens.
- Add the products.

② a 4-digit number ÷ a 2-digit number

```
        104 R6
    25)2606
       25
      ──────
       106
       100
      ──────
         6
```

Steps:
- Divide the hundreds.
- Bring down the tens. Divide the tens.
- Bring down the ones. Divide the ones.
- Write the remainder.

Find the products.

⑥
```
    523
  x  14
```

⑦
```
    278
  x  36
```

⑧
```
    901
  x  49
```

⑨
```
    645
  x  28
```

Find the quotients.

⑩ 13)598

⑪ 27)4914

⑫ 36)1408

⑬ 13)5908

6

Estimate the answers by rounding each number to the nearest thousand. Then find the exact answers.

		Estimate	Answer
⑭	2398 + 1081 + 3008	_____ + _____ + _____ = _____	
⑮	5999 + 2198 + 991	_____ + _____ + _____ = _____	
⑯	12 345 – 1128	_____ – _____ = _____	
⑰	17 409 – 5280	_____ – _____ = _____	

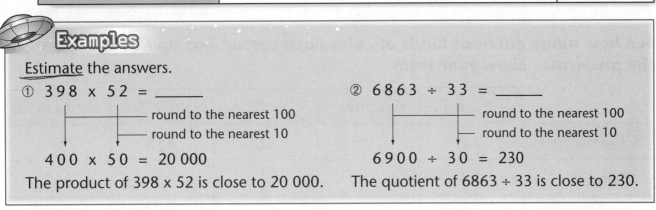

Examples

Estimate the answers.

① 398 x 52 = _____
  — round to the nearest 100
  — round to the nearest 10
  400 x 50 = 20 000
The product of 398 x 52 is close to 20 000.

② 6863 ÷ 33 = _____
  — round to the nearest 100
  — round to the nearest 10
  6900 ÷ 30 = 230
The quotient of 6863 ÷ 33 is close to 230.

Estimate the products first by rounding the numbers to the nearest 10 or 100. Then find the exact answers.

⑱ 19 x 499 = _____   **Estimate** : _____ x _____ = _____

⑲ 208 x 21 = _____   **Estimate** : _____ x _____ = _____

⑳ 384 x 42 = _____   **Estimate** : _____ x _____ = _____

Estimate the quotients first by rounding the numbers to the nearest 10 or 100. Then find the exact answers.

㉑ 5980 ÷ 52 = _____   **Estimate** : _____ ÷ _____ = _____

㉒ 2988 ÷ 19 = _____   **Estimate** : _____ ÷ _____ = _____

㉓ 4126 ÷ 38 = _____   **Estimate** : _____ ÷ _____ = _____

Estimate the following products and put a check mark ✔ in the circle for those products between 5000 and 6000.

㉔ Ⓐ 498 x 15 ◯   Ⓑ 198 x 19 ◯   Ⓒ 501 x 11 ◯

   Ⓓ 230 x 34 ◯   Ⓔ 292 x 18 ◯   Ⓕ 149 x 38 ◯

   Ⓖ 21 x 251 ◯   Ⓗ 98 x 59 ◯   Ⓘ 61 x 103 ◯

Calculate. Use the correct order of operations.

㉕　51 + 92 − 2 x 12

　　= 51 + 92 − _____

　　= _____

㉖　123 + 51 ÷ 3 − 94

　　= 123 + _____ − 94

　　= _____

Quick Tip

For mixed operations, do x or ÷ first, and then do + or −.

㉗　15 x 20 + 17 x 2

　　= _____

　　= _____

㉘　32 x 16 − 28 ÷ 7

　　= _____

　　= _____

㉙　63 ÷ 9 + 45 x 8

　　= _____

　　= _____

See how many different kinds of coins each person has and help them solve the problems. Show your work.

	Ming	Susanna	Sam	Uncle Bill	Aunt Elaine
Quarter	12	108	56	458	0
Dime	15	0	0	0	192
Nickel	13	0	0	0	0

㉚　How much does Ming have?

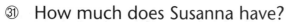

　　She has _____ ¢.

㉛　How much does Susanna have?

　　She has _____ ¢.

㉜　Sam wants to change all his quarters into dimes. How many dimes can he get?

　　He can get _____ dimes.

㉝　How much more money does Uncle Bill have than Aunt Elaine?

　　Uncle Bill has _____ ¢ more than Aunt Elaine.

Keith loves to eat chocolate eggs. Help him solve the problems. Show your work.

㉞ Keith eats 12 chocolate eggs every day. How many chocolate eggs does he eat in a year with 365 days?

$$\begin{array}{r} 365 \\ \times\ 12 \\ \hline 730 \\ 365\ \\ \hline 4380 \end{array}$$

㉟ If one box contains 50 eggs, about how many boxes of chocolate eggs will Keith eat in a normal year?

㊱ Each small bag contains 58 chocolate eggs. Each big bag contains 96 chocolate eggs. Keith has 3 small bags and 2 big bags of chocolate eggs. How many chocolate eggs does he have in all?

㊲ Keith fills a jar with 2858 chocolate eggs for his friends to guess the number of chocolate eggs in it. Carol guesses 2732, Sarah guesses 2586, Oscar guesses 3726, Dave guesses 2866, and Stan guesses 3277. Whose guess is the closest?

㊳ The winner of the game divides the chocolate eggs into 30 bags. About how many chocolate eggs does each bag contain?

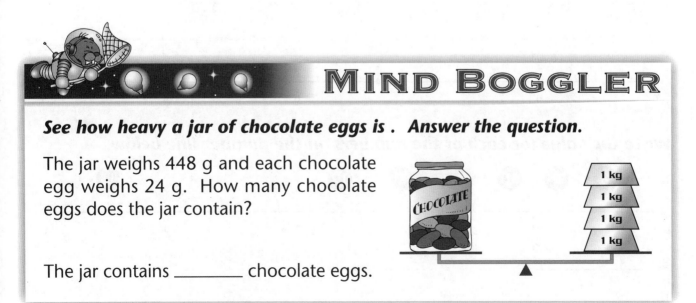

MIND BOGGLER

See how heavy a jar of chocolate eggs is. Answer the question.

The jar weighs 448 g and each chocolate egg weighs 24 g. How many chocolate eggs does the jar contain?

The jar contains _____ chocolate eggs.

2 Decimals

Example

Standard form	Expanded form
24.529	= 20 + 4 + 0.5 + 0.02 + 0.009

In words : Twenty-four and five hundred twenty-nine thousandths

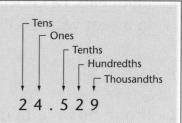

Tens — Ones — Tenths — Hundredths — Thousandths

2 4 . 5 2 9

Write each decimal number in expanded form and in words.

① 257.128   Expanded form : 2 hundreds + 5 tens + 7 ones + 1 tenth + 2 hundredths 8 thosandths

Words : 2 hundred and fifty-seven, one hundred and twenty eight twenty-eigth thosandths.

② 351.082   Expanded form : 3 hundreds + 5 tens + 1 ones + 8 hundredths + 2 thosandths

Words : _____

For the numbers given in expanded form, write them in standard form.

③ 5000 + 400 + 6 + 0.9 + 0.003 = _54.903_

④ 600 + 20 + 0.5 + 0.08 = _62.580_

Put each group of numbers in order from least to greatest using <.

⑤ 59.01   59.15   59.1   59.05   59.01 < 59.05 < 59.1 < 59.15

⑥ 15.238   15.304   15.224   15.322   15.224 < 15.238 < 15.304 < 15.322

Place the following decimal numbers on the number line below.

⑦ | 0.42 | 0.4 | 0.05 | 0.35 | 0.18 | 0.29 | 0.09 |

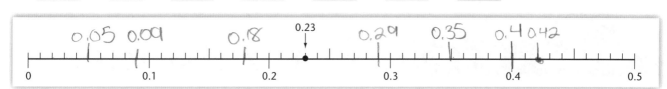

0.05 0.09   0.8   0.23   0.29   0.35   0.40 42

0   0.1   0.2   0.3   0.4   0.5

Write the value for each of the numbers on the number line below.

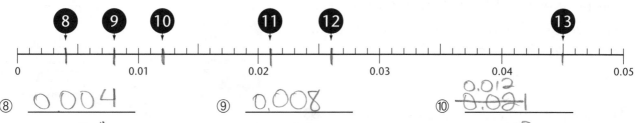

8 9 10   11 12   13

0   0.01   0.02   0.03   0.04   0.05

⑧ _0.004_   ⑨ _0.008_   ⑩ 0.012 ~~0.021~~

⑪ _0.024_   ⑫ _0.026_   ⑬ _0.045_

Add or subtract.

⑭ 28.46 + 21.59 = _____

⑮ 8.63 – 2.47 = _____

⑯ 12.95 – 1.08 = _____

⑰ 6.4 + 4.73 = _____

⑱ 3.745 – 2.339 = _____

⑲ 0.895 + 3.277 = _____

⑳ 4.26 – 3.954 = _____

㉑ 4.815 + 9.69 = _____

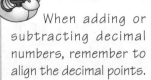

Quick Tip

When adding or subtracting decimal numbers, remember to align the decimal points.

Examples

① 159.63 x 10 = 1596.3 ←— Move the decimal point 1 place to the right.

↑
1 zero

159.63 x 100 = 15963 ←— Move the decimal point 2 places to the right.

↑
2 zeros

② 12.3 x 200
= 12.3 x 100 x 2 ←— Write 200 as 100x2.
= 1230 x 2 ←— Multiply the decimal number by 100.
= 2460

Find the products mentally.

㉒ 29.36 x 100 = 2936

㉓ 58.73 x 100 = 5873

㉔ 139.05 x 10 = 1390.5

㉕ 91.64 x 1000 = 91640

㉖ 25.11 x 1000 = 25110

㉗ 40.23 x 10 = 402.3

Find the products. Show your work.

㉘ 5.4 x 200 = 5.4 x 100 x 200

= _____

㉙ 8.5 x 90 = 8.5 x 10 x 9

= _____

㉚ 2.35 x 800 = 2.35 x 100 x 8

= _____

㉛ 12.4 x 60 = 12.4 x 10 x 6

= _____

Find the products.

㉜ 63.27 x 9 = _____

㉝ 4.53 x 6 = _____

㉞ 270.63 x 6 = _____

㉟ 162.59 x 4 = _____

㊱ 500.092 x 5 = _____

㊲ 327.461 x 7 = _____

㊳ 45.631 x 8 = _____

㊴ 88.64 x 3 = _____

Quick Tip

When multiplying a decimal number and a whole number, remember to place the decimal point in the product.

e.g.

25.4 ←— 1 decimal place

x   2

50.8 ←— 1 decimal place

Examples

① $392.6 \div 10 = 39.26$ ←——— Move the decimal point 1 place to the left.

↑ 1 zero

$392.6 \div 100 = 3.92$ ←——— Move the decimal point 2 places to the left.

↑ 2 zeros

②

Put a decimal point in the quotient above the one in the dividend.

```
     98.09
  4 ) 392.36
      36
      32
      32
        36
        36
```

Don't forget to put a zero in the quotient as a place holder.

Find the quotients mentally.

㊽ $58.23 \div 10 = $ ___5.823___

㊶ $251.3 \div 100 = $ ___2.513___

㊷ $246.5 \div 100 = $ ___2.465___

㊸ $425 \div 100 = $ ___4.25___

㊹ $285.9 \div 10 = $ ___28.59___

㊺ $239.4 \div 10 = $ ___23.94___

Find the quotients.

㊻
```
     03.87
  6 ) 23.22
      18
       52
       48
       42
       42
       00
```

㊼
```
     047.5
  9 ) 427.5
      36
       67
       63
        45
        45
        00
```

㊽
```
     030.18
  7 ) 211.26
      21
       00 12
         7
         56
         56
```

㊾
```
     12.08
  8 ) 96.64
      8
      16
      16
        64
        64
        00
```

㊿ $9.232 \div 8 = $ _____

㊾ $37.41 \div 5 = $ _____

㊾ $30.092 \div 4 = $ _____

㊾ $20.64 \div 3 = $ _____

㊾ $28.609 \div 7 = $ _____

㊾ $38.506 \div 2 = $ _____

Estimate the answers in the shaded boxes. Put a check mark ✔ in the circle if the answer is reasonable; otherwise put a cross X.

㊾ $5.8 \times 7 = $ **406.0** ◯(✓)

㊾ $83.7 \div 6 = $ **13.95** ◯

㊾ $30.9 \div 6 = $ **51.5** ◯

㊾ $10.4 \div 4 = $ **20.6** ◯

㊾ $53.8 \times 3 = $ **161.4** ◯

㊾ $100.3 \div 10 = $ **10.03** ◯

Quick Tip

Round the numbers to the nearest whole number in order to estimate the answers.

12

Look at the flyer. Help Aunt Ann solve the problems.

62. 2 boxes of shortcake weigh __3.94__ kg.

63. 3 boxes of shredded wheat weigh __1.94__ kg.

64. 6 kg of sausages cost $ __26.04__ .

65. 4 bags of apples cost $ __9.96__ .

66. A pack of corned beef has 5 slices. 1 slice of corned beef costs $ __1.07__ .

67. Aunt Ann pays 9 quarters for 1 <u>bag</u> of <u>apples</u>. How much more does <u>she</u> need to pay?

$$
\begin{array}{r}
9.96 \\
- 3.00 \\
\hline
6.96 \leftarrow
\end{array}
$$

68. Aunt Ann wants to buy 3 kg of sausages and 2 kg of grapes. How much does she need to pay?

Sausage
$$
\begin{array}{r}
14.34 \\
\times 3 \\
\hline
13.02
\end{array}
$$

Grapes
$$
\begin{array}{r}
3.24 \\
\times 2 \\
\hline
6.48
\end{array}
$$

$$
\begin{array}{r}
13.02 \\
+ 6.48 \\
\hline
19.50 \leftarrow
\end{array}
$$

69. Aunt Ann buys 1 box of shredded wheat and divides the wheat equally into 3 portions. How many kg of shredded wheat are there in each portion?

$$
\begin{array}{r}
0.165 \\
3 \overline{)0.495} \\
3 \\
\hline
19 \\
18 \\
\hline
015 \\
15 \\
\hline
00
\end{array}
$$

a6 0.165

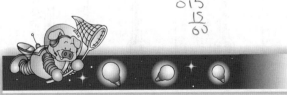

MIND BOGGLER

There are 2 boxes of shortcake and 3 packs of corned beef in the basket. If the total weight of the basket and the food is 3.085 kg, how many kilograms does the basket weigh?

The basket weighs _____ kg.

3 Integers and Number Theory

Examples

① Negative integers are used commonly:

- -20°C ← 20°C below 0°C
- -100 m ← 100 m below sea level
- -$200 ← $200 withdrawn

② If the temperature changes from 4°C to -2°C, it drops 6°C in all.

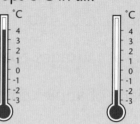

Write the value for each of the letters on the number line below.

①

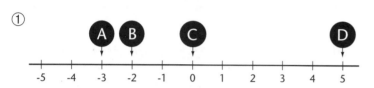

A _____ B _____

C _____ D _____

Circle the larger number in each pair of integers.

② -4 3	③ -3 -5	④ 2 -2	⑤ 0 -1
⑥ -3 1	⑦ -2 -3	⑧ 0 -5	⑨ -4 4

Record the temperature for each day. Then answer the questions.

⑩

SUN	MON	TUE	WED	THU	FRI	SAT
°C 4 3 2 1 0 -1 -2 -3 -4	°C 4 3 2 1 0 -1 -2 -3 -4	°C 4 3 2 1 0 -1 -2 -3 -4	°C 4 3 2 1 0 -1 -2 -3 -4	°C 4 3 2 1 0 -1 -2 -3 -4	°C 4 3 2 1 0 -1 -2 -3 -4	°C 4 3 2 1 0 -1 -2 -3 -4

⑪ Which day was colder, Sunday or Thursday? _____

⑫ Which day was the warmest? _____

⑬ In how many days was the temperature above 1°C? _____ days

⑭ On which day was the temperature 2°C higher than that on Monday? _____

14

Look at the 50-square chart and complete the following questions.

1	2	3	4	5	6	7	8	9	10
11	12	13	14	15	16	17	18	19	20
21	22	23	24	25	26	27	28	29	30
31	32	33	34	35	36	37	38	39	40
41	42	43	44	45	46	47	48	49	50

⑮ Circle the multiples of 4.

⑯ Cross the multiples of 6.

⑰ Colour the mutiples of 5 grey.

⑱ Numbers with ⬤ are common multiples of 4 and _____ . They are _____ .

⑲ Numbers with ⊗ are common multiples of 4 and _____ . They are _____

_____ .

⑳ The least common multiple (L.C.M.) of 4 and 5 is _____ .

㉑ The least common multiple (L.C.M.) of 4 and 6 is _____ .

Write the first 10 multiples of each number.

> **Quick Tip**
>
> Multiples of a number can be obtained by multiplying the number by 1, 2, 3, ... and so on. The smallest common multiple of a group of numbers is their least common multiple (L.C.M.).

㉒ 3 _____

㉓ 5 _____

㉔ 8 _____

㉕ 10 _____

Refer to question ㉒ to ㉕. List the first three common multiples of each group of numbers and write their least common multiple (L.C.M.).

		3 and 5	3 and 8	5 and 8	5 and 10
㉖	Common multiples				
㉗	L.C.M.				

Find the factors of each number and complete the sentences.

㉘ 12 = 1 x _____
   = 2 x _____
   = 3 x _____
   The factors of 12 :
   _____

㉙ 20 ÷ 1 = _____
   20 ÷ 2 = _____
   20 ÷ 4 = _____
   The factors of 20 :
   _____

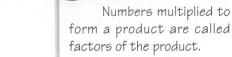

> **Quick Tip**
>
> Numbers multiplied to form a product are called factors of the product.
>
> You can use multiplication or division to find the factors of a number.

㉚ The common factors of 12 and 20 are _____ .

The greatest common factor of 12 and 20 is _____ .

15

Find the factors of each number. List the common factors of each group of numbers and write their greatest common factor (G.C.F.).

			Common factors	G.C.F.
㉛	16 _____	18 _____		
㉜	15 _____	30 _____		
㉝	10 _____	24 _____		

Circle the prime numbers.

㉞

2	3	63	29	16	25	97
19	87	73	77	51	23	46
32	31	11	24	67	13	81

Quick Tip

Any number with only 1 and itself as factors is called a prime number. Numbers which are not prime are called composite numbers. 1 is neither a prime nor a composite number.

Example

Write 36 as a product of prime factors.

Factor tree

$$36$$
$$4 \times 9$$
$$2 \times 2 \times 3 \times 3 \leftarrow \text{prime numbers}$$

$36 = 2 \times 2 \times 3 \times 3$

Quick Tip

The number "1" is not used in factor trees.

Complete the factor trees and write each number as a product of prime factors.

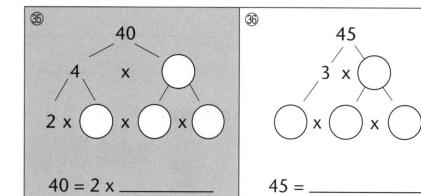

㉟

40
4 x ◯
2 x ◯ x ◯ x ◯

40 = 2 x _____

㊱

45
3 x ◯
◯ x ◯ x ◯

45 = _____

㊲

56
4 x ◯
2 x ◯ x ◯ x ◯

56 = _____

㊳ 72 = _____

㊴ 32 = _____

㊵ 60 = _____

㊶ 50 = _____

㊷ 54 = _____

㊸ 80 = _____

Example

Determine the G.C.F. and L.C.M. of 30 and 50.

common factors

product of common factors

```
      30                    50
     /  \                  /  \
    2  x 15               2  x 25
        / \                   / \
  2  x  3 x 5        2  x   5 x 5
```

$30 = \boxed{2} \times 3 \times \boxed{5}$
$50 = \boxed{2} \quad\quad \times \boxed{5} \times 5$

product of common factors

G.C.F. $= 2 \quad\quad \times 5 \quad = 10$ ← product of common factors and other factors
L.C.M. $= 2 \times 3 \times 5 \times 5 = 150$ ←

Write each number as a product of prime factors. Then determine the G.C.F. and L.C.M. of each group of numbers.

㊹ 21 = _____

28 = _____

G.C.F. = _____ L.C.M. = _____

㊺ 16 = _____

24 = _____

G.C.F. = _____ L.C.M. = _____

Complete the calculation.

㊻ 7 x (3 + 4)

= 7 x ____ + 7 x ____

= ____ + ____

= ____

㊼ 12 x (7 – 2)

= 12 x ____ – 12 x ____

= ____ – ____

= ____

Quick Tip

Distributive property of multiplication:

$5 \times (10 + 6) = 5 \times 10 + 5 \times 6$
$\quad\quad\quad\quad\quad = 50 + 30$
$\quad\quad\quad\quad\quad = 80$

㊽ 9 x 27

= 9 x (20 + 7)

= 9 x ____ + 9 x ____

= ____ + ____

= ____

㊾ 8 x 49

= 8 x (50 – 1)

= 8 x ____ – 8 x ____

= ____ – ____

= ____

㊿ 5 x 98

= 5 x (100 – ____)

= 5 x ____ – 5 x ____

= ____ – ____

= ____

MIND BOGGLER

Add or subtract. Then write even or odd to complete the sentences.

① 10 + 24 = ____   The sum of 2 even numbers is _____ .

② 37 – 15 = ____   The difference between 2 odd numbers is _____ .

③ 36 – 11 = ____   The difference between an even and an odd number is

_____ .

4 Percent

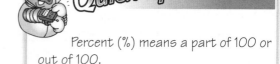
Rewrite the following percents using %.

① sixty-nine percent = _____

② one hundred percent = _____

③ 8 out of 100 = _____

④ 26 out of 100 = _____

⑤ $\frac{42}{100}$ = _____

⑥ $\frac{7}{100}$ = _____

⑦ $\frac{83}{100}$ = _____

⑧ $\frac{98}{100}$ = _____

Write the percent that represents the shaded part of each 100-square grid.

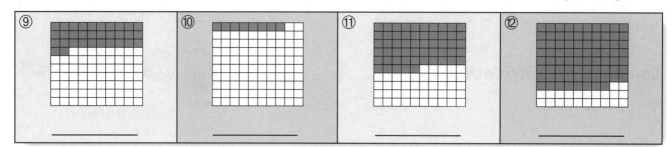

⑨   _____

⑩   _____

⑪   _____

⑫   _____

Colour each 100-square grid according to the given percent.

⑬   62%

⑭   24%

⑮   7%

⑯   91%

Look at the shapes. Then fill in the blanks.

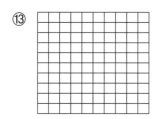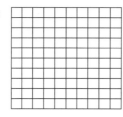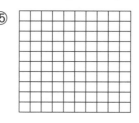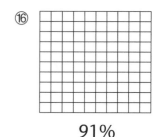

⑰ There are _____ stars. _____ out of 100 shapes are stars. _____ % of the shapes are stars.

⑱ There are _____ circles. _____ out of 100 shapes are circles. _____ % of the shapes are circles.

⑲ There are _____ hearts. _____ out of 100 shapes are hearts. _____ % of the shapes are hearts.

Estimate the percent of the line segment represented by each mark.

㉒

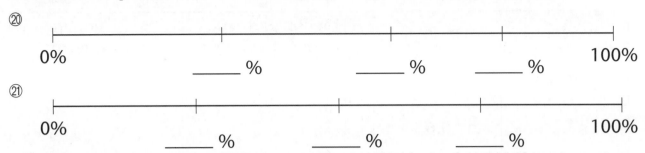

0%   _____ %   _____ %   _____ %   100%

㉑

0%   _____ %   _____ %   _____ %   100%

Complete the following fractions and find the percents. Fill in the boxes.

 Example

Joshi gets 37 out of 50 on a test. What is his test percentage?

$37 \text{ out of } 50 = \dfrac{37}{50} = \dfrac{37 \times 2}{50 \times 2} = \dfrac{74}{100} = 74\%$ ⟵ Write an equivalent fraction with 100 in the denominator.

㉒ $\dfrac{43}{50} = \dfrac{}{100} = \boxed{} \%$ ㉓ $\dfrac{17}{20} = \dfrac{}{100} = \boxed{} \%$

㉔ $\dfrac{9}{10} = \dfrac{}{100} = \boxed{} \%$ ㉕ $\dfrac{130}{200} = \dfrac{}{100} = \boxed{} \%$

㉖ $\dfrac{23}{25} = \dfrac{}{100} = \boxed{} \%$ ㉗ $\dfrac{340}{400} = \dfrac{}{100} = \boxed{} \%$

Write each percent as fraction in lowest terms.

㉘ 20% = _____ ㉙ 25% = _____ ㉚ 50% = _____

㉛ 75% = _____ ㉜ 82% = _____ ㉝ 8% = _____

㉞ 16% = _____ ㉟ 33% = _____ ㊱ 200% = _____

Rewrite the following percents as decimals.

㊲ 26% = _____ ㊳ 37% = _____

㊴ 95% = _____ ㊵ 66% = _____

㊶ 9% = _____ ㊷ 74% = _____

 **Quick Tip**

Write percents as fractions with 100 in the denominator first. Then write the fractions as decimals.

Circle the fraction closest in value to each percent.

㊸ 10% $\dfrac{1}{5}$ $\dfrac{1}{8}$ ㊹ 80% $\dfrac{19}{25}$ $\dfrac{3}{4}$

㊺ 66% $\dfrac{7}{10}$ $\dfrac{3}{5}$ ㊻ 43% $\dfrac{1}{2}$ $\dfrac{9}{20}$

Complete the table.

	Percent	Decimal	Fraction with 100 as denominator	Fraction in lowest terms
㊼	70%			
㊽		0.6		
㊾			$\frac{45}{100}$	
㊿				$\frac{1}{20}$

Choose and write the percent that comes between each pair of numbers.

7%	78%	26%	52%	86%	11%

(51) 0.13 ________ $\frac{2}{5}$

(52) 0.8 ________ $\frac{3}{4}$

(53) $\frac{4}{5}$ ________ 0.92

(54) $\frac{2}{3}$ ________ 0.45

(55) $\frac{1}{20}$ ________ 0.2

(56) $\frac{1}{20}$ ________ 0.09

Write each group of numbers in order from least to greatest.

(57) $\frac{19}{50}$ 0.27 59% ______________________________

(58) 0.93 64% $\frac{18}{25}$ ______________________________

(59) 71% $\frac{3}{4}$ 0.73 ______________________________

Complete the following fractions and statements.

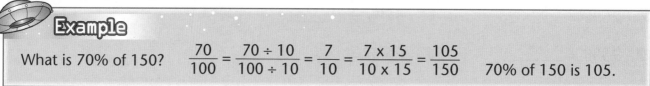

Example

What is 70% of 150? $\frac{70}{100} = \frac{70 \div 10}{100 \div 10} = \frac{7}{10} = \frac{7 \times 15}{10 \times 15} = \frac{105}{150}$ 70% of 150 is 105.

(60) $\frac{25}{100} = \frac{\quad}{300}$

25% of 300 is ________ .

(61) $\frac{70}{100} = \frac{\quad}{50}$

70% of 50 is ________ .

(62) $\frac{93}{100} = \frac{\quad}{200}$

93% of 200 is ________ .

(63) $\frac{55}{100} = \frac{\quad}{20}$

55% of 20 is ________ .

See how many cookies are in each group or each child has. Use % to complete each sentence and answer the questions.

64

a. _____ of the cookies are chocolate chip cookies.

b. _____ of the cookies are raisin cookies.

c. _____ of the cookies are ginger cookies.

d. _____ of the cookies are in bags.

e. _____ of the cookies are in boxes.

65

a. _____ of the cookies are chocolate chip cookies.

b. _____ of the cookies are ginger cookies.

c. Uncle Sam has a bag of ginger cookies and he eats 20 of them. He eats _____ of the ginger cookies.

d. Sue has a bag of chocolate chip cookies and she eats 4 of them. She eats _____ of the chocolate chip cookies.

66 Tim has a box of 30 cookies; he eats 18 cookies. Ray has a box of 25 cookies; he eats 16 cookies. What percent of the cookies does each child eat? Who has eaten the higher percent of cookies?

MIND BOGGLER

Read what Edmond says. Then tell why he is incorrect.

I have 100 marbles. There are the same number of marbles in each of the 4 colours. Each colour makes up 26% of the marbles.

_____

5 Fractions

Change each of the following improper fractions to mixed numbers and then find the message below by matching the letters with the mixed numbers.

① $\frac{3}{2}$ **I** _____ ② $\frac{9}{5}$ **E** _____

Quick Tip

Use division to convert an improper fraction to a mixed number.

e.g. $\frac{9}{5} = 1\frac{4}{5}$ $\begin{array}{r} 1 \\ 5\overline{)9} \\ 5 \\ \hline 4 \end{array}$

③ $\frac{17}{6}$ **M** _____ ④ $\frac{13}{6}$ **K** _____

⑤ $\frac{5}{4}$ **F** _____ ⑥ $\frac{13}{2}$ **P** _____

⑦ $\frac{29}{18}$ **C** _____ ⑧ $\frac{11}{5}$ **R** _____ ⑨ $\frac{7}{3}$ **T** _____

⑩ $\frac{7}{6}$ **D** _____ ⑪ $\frac{25}{18}$ **S** _____ ⑫ $\frac{23}{18}$ **A** _____

⑬ $6\frac{1}{2}$ $2\frac{1}{5}$ $1\frac{5}{18}$ $1\frac{11}{18}$ $2\frac{1}{3}$ $1\frac{1}{2}$ $1\frac{11}{18}$ $1\frac{4}{5}$ $2\frac{5}{6}$ $1\frac{5}{18}$ $2\frac{1}{6}$ $1\frac{4}{5}$ $1\frac{7}{18}$

$6\frac{1}{2}$ $1\frac{4}{5}$ $2\frac{1}{5}$ $1\frac{1}{4}$ $1\frac{4}{5}$ $1\frac{11}{18}$ $2\frac{1}{3}$!

Put the following fractions in order from least to greatest using <.

⑭ $\frac{5}{8}$ $\frac{7}{8}$ $\frac{4}{8}$ _____

⑮ $\frac{9}{10}$ $\frac{9}{7}$ $\frac{9}{4}$ _____

⑯ $2\frac{4}{5}$ $3\frac{1}{5}$ $2\frac{3}{5}$ _____

⑰ $1\frac{5}{6}$ $1\frac{1}{6}$ $2\frac{5}{6}$ _____

Quick Tip

Fractions with the same denominator
The larger the numerator, the greater the value,
e.g. $\frac{2}{8} < \frac{5}{8}$

Fractions with the same numerator
The larger the denominator, the smaller the value,
e.g. $\frac{5}{9} < \frac{5}{4}$

Circle the smaller fraction in each pair.

⑱ $\frac{5}{2}$ $\frac{17}{6}$ ⑲ $\frac{7}{3}$ $\frac{8}{5}$ ⑳ $1\frac{1}{8}$ $\frac{13}{12}$

㉑ $\frac{13}{4}$ $\frac{17}{5}$ ㉒ $\frac{8}{3}$ $\frac{15}{6}$ ㉓ $\frac{12}{5}$ $\frac{5}{2}$

㉔ $\frac{23}{8}$ $\frac{16}{6}$ ㉕ $\frac{17}{4}$ $\frac{9}{2}$ ㉖ $\frac{11}{3}$ $\frac{16}{7}$

Quick Tip

Steps to compare fractions :
1st: Write the fractions as mixed numbers.
2nd: Compare the whole numbers. If they are the same, go to 3rd step.
3rd: Compare the fractions. Write the fractions with the same denominator and then compare their numerators.

Use fractions to write each addition or subtraction sentence. Write the answer in lowest terms.

 Examples

①

$$\frac{3}{8} + \frac{1}{8} = \frac{4}{8} = \frac{1}{2}$$

②

$$\frac{7}{8} - \frac{3}{8} = \frac{4}{8} = \frac{1}{2}$$

㉗ [   ] + [   ] = [   ]

_____ + _____ = _____

㉘ [   ] + [   ] = [   ] = [   ]

_____ + _____ = _____ = _____

㉙ [   ] − [   ] = [   ]

_____ − _____ = _____

㉚ [   ] − [   ] = [   ] = [   ]

_____ − _____ = _____ = _____

Find the sums or differences. Reduce the answers to lowest terms.

㉛ $\dfrac{17}{18} - \dfrac{11}{18} =$ _____ = _____

㉜ $\dfrac{11}{20} + \dfrac{3}{20} =$ _____ = _____

㉝ $\dfrac{23}{30} + \dfrac{7}{30} =$ _____ = _____

㉞ $\dfrac{2}{15} + \dfrac{4}{15} =$ _____ = _____

㉟ $\dfrac{11}{25} + \dfrac{9}{25} =$ _____ = _____

㊱ $\dfrac{25}{42} - \dfrac{13}{42} =$ _____ = _____

㊲ $\dfrac{7}{12} - \dfrac{5}{12} =$ _____ = _____

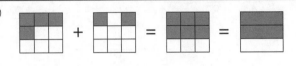 *Quick Tip*

When adding or subtracting fractions with the same denominator, add or subtract the numerators. Remember to reduce the answers to lowest terms.

Use fractions to write each addition or subtraction sentence. Write each answer in lowest terms.

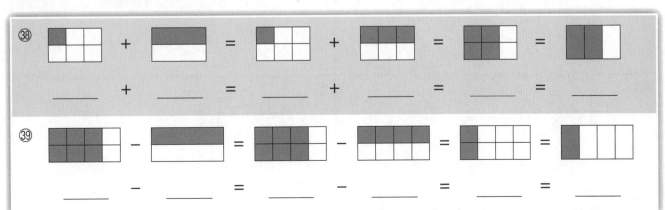

㊳ [   ] + [   ] = [   ] + [   ] = [   ] = [   ]

_____ + _____ = _____ + _____ = _____ = _____

㊴ [   ] − [   ] = [   ] − [   ] = [   ] = [   ]

_____ − _____ = _____ − _____ = _____ = _____

Write the numbers. Reduce your answers to lowest terms.

(40) $\frac{1}{3} + \frac{1}{6} = \frac{\ }{6} + \frac{1}{6}$

$= \frac{\ }{6}$

$=$ ______

(41) $\frac{9}{10} - \frac{1}{2} = \frac{9}{10} - \frac{\ }{10}$

$= \frac{\ }{10}$

$=$ ______

(42) $1\frac{3}{4} - \frac{5}{8} = \frac{\ }{4} - \frac{5}{8}$

$= \frac{\ }{8} - \frac{5}{8}$

$= \frac{\ }{8}$

$=$ ______

(43) $\frac{7}{12} + 1\frac{2}{3} = \frac{7}{12} + \frac{\ }{3}$

$= \frac{7}{12} + \frac{\ }{12}$

$= \frac{\ }{12}$

$=$ ______

Quick Tip

Change the mixed numbers to improper fractions first. Then write equivalent fractions with a common denominator before adding or subtracting fractions with unlike denominators.

Add or subtract. Reduce your answers to lowest terms. Show your work.

(44) $\frac{1}{2} + \frac{1}{3} =$

(45) $\frac{3}{5} - \frac{1}{3} =$

(46) $2\frac{1}{3} - \frac{7}{15} =$

(47) $3\frac{5}{6} - 1\frac{1}{4} =$

(48) $1\frac{2}{5} + 2\frac{1}{10} =$

(49) $1\frac{7}{8} + 2\frac{3}{4} =$

(50) $1\frac{3}{4} - \frac{5}{8} =$

(51) $3\frac{1}{3} - 2\frac{1}{4} =$

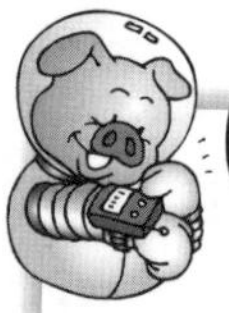

Look at the kinds of nuts the children have and answer the questions. Write all the fractions in lowest terms.

Steve		Stan		Bob	
pistachios	$\frac{4}{5}$ kg	pistachios	$1\frac{1}{2}$ kg	walnuts	$\frac{7}{8}$ kg
walnuts	$1\frac{3}{8}$ kg	walnuts	$3\frac{1}{6}$ kg	peanuts	$1\frac{1}{6}$ kg
pecans	$2\frac{2}{3}$ kg	pecans	$\frac{7}{12}$ kg	pecans	$1\frac{1}{3}$ kg

52 How many kilograms of walnuts do Steve and Bob have? _____ kg

53 How many kilograms of pecans do Steve and Bob have? _____ kg

54 How many more kilograms of walnuts does Steve have than Bob? _____ kg

55 How many kilograms of pistachios do Steve and Stan have? _____ kg

56 How many kilograms of pecans do Stan and Bob have? _____ kg

57 How many more kilograms of pecans does Steve have than Stan? _____ kg

58 How many kilograms of nuts does Stan have? _____ kg

59 How many kilograms of nuts does Bob have? _____ kg

60 How many more kilograms of nuts does Stan have than Bob? _____ kg

61 Steve puts his pistachios into 2 bags. 1 bag weighs $\frac{2}{15}$ kg. How heavy is the other bag? _____ kg

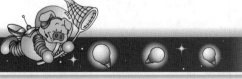

MIND BOGGLER

See how Stan and Bob trade their nuts.

Every $\frac{1}{3}$ kg of pecans can be traded for $\frac{1}{4}$ kg of pistachios. How many kilograms of pistachios can I get if I trade all my pecans to Stan?

Bob

Bob can get _____ kg of pistachios if he trades all his pecans to Stan.

6 Rate and Ratio

Example

Jim runs 14 km in 2 hours. At what rate does he run?

Rate: $14 \div 2 = 7$

His rate is 7 km/h (7 km per hour).

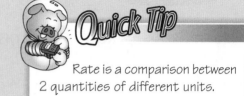

Quick Tip

Rate is a comparison between 2 quantities of different units.

Find the rates.

① 50 words in 20 min _____ words/min

② 80 km in 4 h _____ km/h

③ 300 words in 5 min _____ words/min

④ 48 km in 8 h _____ km/h

⑤ 25 boxes for $75.00 $ _____ /box

⑥ $24 for 6 h $ _____ /h

⑦ 5 boxes for $12.50 $ _____ /box

⑧ $126 for 9 h $ _____ /h

⑨ $ 2.00	⑩ SOUP $ 9.60	⑪ 2 kg $ 8.54
$ _____ /orange	$ _____ /can	$ _____ /kg

Find the unit price for each item sold in each store. Then tell which store offers the best buy.

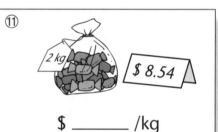

		Store A	Store B	Store C	Best buy
⑫	Chicken breast	$19.80 for 3 kg $ ____ /kg	$25.80 for 4 kg $ ____ /kg	$34.25 for 5 kg $ ____ /kg	Store
⑬	Spring Water	3 bottles for $3.57 $ ____ /bottle	4 bottles for $5.00 $ ____ /bottle	2 bottles for $2.84 $ ____ /bottle	Store
⑭	Cup Noodles	5 cups for $3.95 $ ____ /cup	2 cups for $1.36 $ ____ /cup	3 cups for $2.67 $ ____ /cup	Store

Example

There are 4 girls and 6 boys. What is the ratio of the number of girls to the number of boys?

No. of girls : No. of boys = 4 : 6 $(4:6 = \frac{4}{6} = \frac{4 \div 2}{6 \div 2} = \frac{2}{3} = 2:3)$

$\qquad\qquad\qquad\qquad = 2 : 3$ (4:6 and 2:3 are equivalent ratios.)

The ratio of the number of girls to the number of boys is 2 : 3.

Quick Tip

Ratio is a comparison between 2 or more quantities of the same unit. A ratio can be written in fraction form,

e.g. $2 : 3 = \frac{2}{3}$

Write 2 equivalent ratios for each ratio.

⑮   5 : 7   _____   _____   ⑯   4 : 9   _____   _____

⑰   10 : 15   _____   _____   ⑱   12 : 20   _____   _____

Write each ratio in lowest terms.

⑲   75 : 25   _____   ⑳   20 : 80   _____   ㉑   85 : 15   _____

㉒   28 : 72   _____   ㉓   32 : 48   _____   ㉔   30 : 25   _____

Look at the fruits. Write each ratio in lowest terms.

㉕   apples to bananas   = _____

㉖   bananas to oranges   = _____

㉗   apples to fruits   = _____

㉘   oranges to fruits   = _____

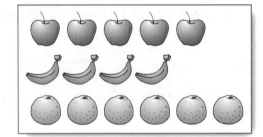

Complete the table.

	Ratio	Fraction	Decimal	Percent
㉙	9 : 25			
㉚		$\frac{2}{5}$		
㉛			0.82	
㉜				65%
㉝			0.15	

Quick Tip

Use division to convert a fraction to a decimal.

To convert a decimal to a percent, multiply the decimal by 100 and add %,

e.g. 0.17 = 0.17 x 100%

$\qquad\qquad$ = 17%

Lucy has a sheet of stickers. Look at Lucy's stickers and answer the questions. Write the ratios in lowest terms.

㉞ polar bears : teddy bears = _____

㉟ parrots : eagles = _____

㊱ polar bears : eagles = _____

㊲ teddy bears : bears = _____

㊳ polar bears : bears = _____

㊴ parrots : birds = _____

㊵ eagles : birds = _____

㊶ bears : all stickers = _____

㊷ birds : all stickers = _____

㊸ 2 sheets of stickers cost $3.24. What is the cost of 1 sheet of stickers?

_____

㊹ How much do 4 sheets of stickers cost?

_____

㊺ Lucy sells her stickers at the price of 6¢/sticker. If Amanda buys 8 stickers from Lucy, how much does she need to pay?

_____

㊻ Randy pays $0.90 to buy some stickers from Lucy. How many stickers does he buy?

_____

㊼ What is the ratio of the number of stickers sold to the number of stickers left?

_____

㊽ Lucy sells all her stickers in 3 days. What is the selling rate?

_____

Solve the problems. Reduce the answers to lowest terms.

㊾ In a bag, there are 8 red balloons, 4 green balloons and 12 blue balloons.

a. What is the ratio of red balloons to green balloons? _____

b. What is the ratio of green balloons to blue balloons? _____

c. If it takes 48 minutes to inflate all the balloons, what is the rate of inflating the balloons? _____

㊿ Sergi takes 2 years to collect 70 hockey cards and 28 baseball cards.

a. What is the ratio of hockey cards to baseball cards? _____

b. What is the rate in cards/year at which Sergi collects his hockey cards? _____

c. If Sergi continues to collect hockey cards at the same rate, how many hockey cards will he have in 5 years? _____

d. What is the rate in cards/year at which Sergi collects his cards? _____

e. If Sergi continues to collect cards at the same rate, how many more cards will he collect over the next 10 years? _____

MIND BOGGLER

Aunt Janet earns $4800 in 2 months. Look at her expenditure. Answer the questions.

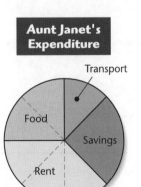

Aunt Janet's Expenditure

Transport
Food
Savings
Rent

① What is Aunt Janet's earning rate? _____

② How much does Aunt Janet spend on rent each month? _____

③ How much does Aunt Janet spend on food each month? _____

④ What is the ratio of the money spent on transport to savings? _____

7 Time, Distance and Speed

Write the 24-hour clock times.

① 4:35 p.m. _____

② 6:12 a.m. _____

③ 11:25:46 a.m. _____

④ 10:42:11 p.m. _____

⑤ 4:27:53 p.m. _____

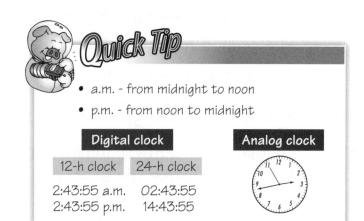

Quick Tip

- a.m. - from midnight to noon
- p.m. - from noon to midnight

Digital clock		Analog clock
12-h clock	24-h clock	
2:43:55 a.m.	02:43:55	
2:43:55 p.m.	14:43:55	

Write the 12-hour clock times in the boxes and draw the clock hands to show the times.

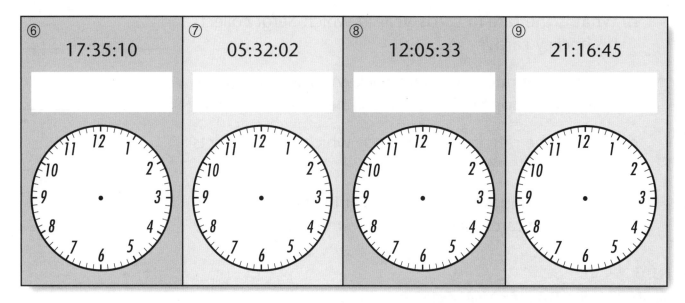

⑥ 17:35:10

⑦ 05:32:02

⑧ 12:05:33

⑨ 21:16:45

Write the 24-hour clock times.

⑩ 3 h before 02:11:20 _____

⑪ 1 h 15 s after 06:30:50 _____

⑫ 2 h 30 s before 15:38:20 _____

Answer the questions.

⑬ Movie A starts at 2:45:16 p.m. and ends at 4:55:51 p.m.
How long does it last? _____

⑭ Joshua goes to bed at 23:15:40 and gets up at 08:00:23
the next morning. How long does he sleep? _____

Fill in the blanks to show the equivalent lengths.

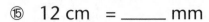

⑮ 12 cm = _____ mm   ⑯ 50 mm = _____ cm

⑰ 8 m   = _____ cm   ⑱ 900 cm = _____ m

⑲ 4 km   = _____ m   ⑳ 2500 m = _____ km

㉑ 8.4 m = _____ cm   ㉒ 66 cm = _____ m   ㉓ 25 mm = _____ cm

㉔ 7500 m = _____ km   ㉕ 3.72 cm = _____ mm   ㉖ 452 cm = _____ m

Fill in the blanks.

| 30 cm | 560 km | 9 mm | 28 m |

㉗ The distance between 2 boys standing at 2 corners of a basketball court is about _____ .

㉘ The distance a cricket can leap is about _____ .

㉙ The distance between the eyes of a snail is about _____ .

㉚ The distance between Toronto and Montreal is about _____ .

Find the closest distance between the places. Then answer the questions.

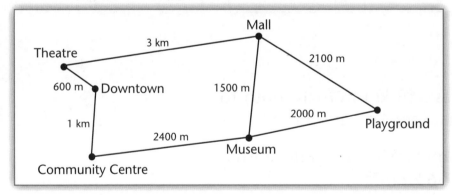

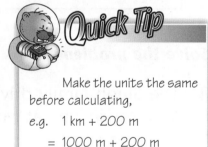

㉛ Theatre to mall : _____ m   ㉜ Museum to playground : _____ km

㉝ Theatre to downtown : _____ km   ㉞ Mall to museum : _____ km

㉟ Playground to community centre passing museum : _____ km

㊱ Museum to theatre via community centre and downtown : _____ km

㊲ Which is the shortest route to travel from downtown to playground? What is the distance?

① Uncle Ron drives 90 km in 2 hours. At what speed does he drive?
Speed : 90 ÷ 2 = 45
He drives at 45 km/h.

② How far can Ted drive in 3 hours at 40 km/h?
Distance : 40 x 3 = 120
He can drive 120 km.

③ How long does Pat take to drive 50 km at 20 km/h?
Time : 50 ÷ 20 = 2.5
He takes 2.5 hours.

Complete the table.

	Distance	Time	Speed
㊳	100 km	4 h	
㊴	320 km	5 h	
㊵	25 m	10 s	
㊶		2 h	46 km/h
㊷		3.5 h	20 km/h
㊸	120 m		60 m/s
㊹	125 m		5 m/s

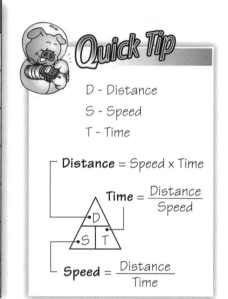

Quick Tip

D - Distance
S - Speed
T - Time

Distance = Speed x Time

Time = Distance / Speed

Speed = Distance / Time

Solve the problems.

㊺ The Singh family drives 560 km from Toronto to Montreal in 7 h. At what speed do they drive? _____

㊻ How long does the Singh family take to drive from Montreal to Toronto at 56 km/h? _____

㊼ Lucy cycles 23 km in 2 h. What is her speed? _____

㊽ How far can Lucy cycle in 4.5 h? _____

㊾ How long does Lucy take to cycle 80.5 km? _____

㊿ Paul cycles 7 km in $\frac{1}{2}$ h and Pat cycles 24 km in 2 h. Who cycles faster? Show your work.

_____ cycles faster.

Look at the records for the Track and Field Day at Riverview School. Complete the tables and solve the problems.

(51) a.

100-m Race			
Place	Start	Finish	Time taken
1st			15 s
2nd			20 s
3rd	10:20:35		25 s
4th			29 s
5th			30 s

b.

1500-m Race			
Place	Start	Finish	Time taken
1st			6 min
2nd			6 min 30 s
3rd	12:05:45		6 min 45 s
4th			6 min 55 s
5th			7 min 10 s

(52) What was the difference in time between the 1st and the 5th place runners in the 100-m race? ____________

(53) What was the difference in time between the start of the 100-m race and the start of the 1500-m race? ____________

(54) Ben can run 100 m in 18 s. How long will it take him to run 200 m at the same speed? ____________

(55) Ben can run 1500 m at half his 100-m speed. How long would he take to run 1500 m? ____________

(56) Sarah can run at a speed of 5 m/s. How far can she run in 20 s? ____________

(57) Pete can run 200 m in 100 s. What is his speed in m/s? ____________

(58) How far in m can Pete run in 1 min at this speed? ____________

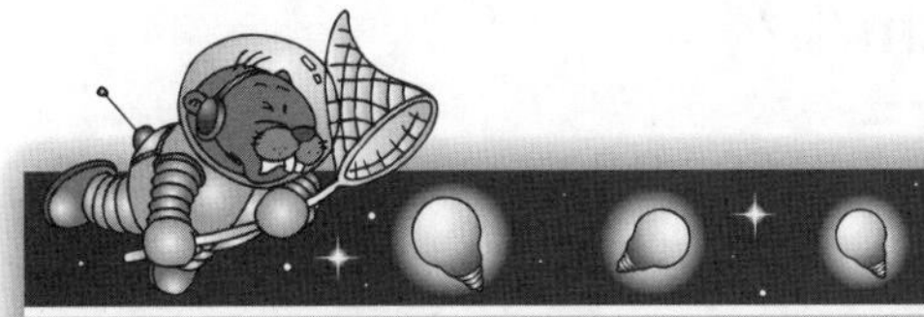

MIND BOGGLER

How many metres more will a car travel in 12 min at a speed of 50 km/h than at a speed of 40 km/h?

It will travel ____________ m more.

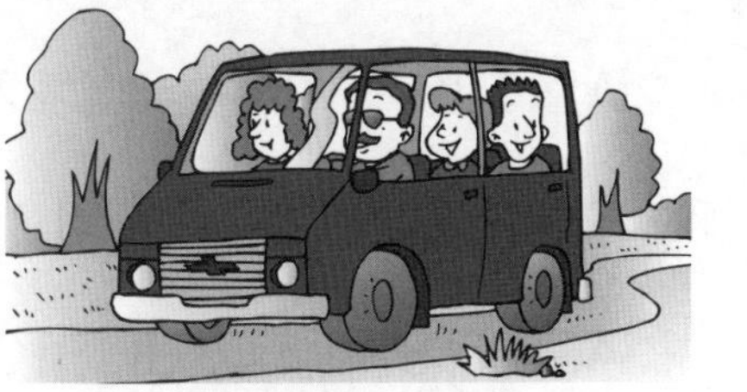

Circle the letter which represents the correct answer in each problem.

① How many prime numbers are there between 1 and 30?

    A. 7   B. 9   C. 10   D. 11

② Which of the following is equal to $5 \times (7 + 9)$?

    A. $5 \times 7 + 9$ B. $5 + 7 \times 9$ C. $5 + 5 \times 9$ D. $35 + 45$

③ The time on a digital clock reads 23:53:50. How long is it till midnight?

    A. 6 min 10 s   B. 6 min 50 s   C. 7 min 10 s   D. 7 min 5 s

④ The greatest common factor (G.C.F.) of 12 and 18 is _____ .

    A. 6   B. 12   C. 18   D. 36

⑤ The least common multiple (L.C.M.) of 12 and 15 is _____ .

    A. 30   B. 60   C. 120   D. 180

⑥ The temperature was -8°C and it increased by 3°C to _____ .

    A. -11°C   B. -5°C   C. 5°C   D. 11°C

⑦ What is the sum of $\frac{5}{6}$ and $\frac{1}{9}$ in lowest terms?

    A. $\frac{6}{15}$ B. $\frac{5}{54}$ C. $\frac{17}{18}$ D. $\frac{51}{54}$

⑧ Which number, when divided by 100, equals 152.3?

    A. 1.523   B. 15.23   C. 1523   D. 15 230

⑨ How many km can you travel in 20 min at 60 km/h?

    A. 12   B. 20   C. 30   D. 80

⑩ What is 15% of $150?

    A. $20   B. $22.50   C. $23   D. $25

⑪ There are 8 boys and 10 girls. What is the ratio of boys to girls?

    A. 8:18   B. 10:18   C. 5:4   D. 4:5

Do the following calculation without a calculator. Show your work.

| ⑫ $\begin{array}{r} 123 \\ \times\ \ 47 \\ \hline \end{array}$ | ⑬ $\begin{array}{r} 342.95 \\ \times\ \ \ \ \ \ 7 \\ \hline \end{array}$ | ⑭ $29\overline{\smash{)}1566}$ | ⑮ $3\overline{\smash{)}25.92}$ |

⑯ 4 x 5.2 x 25	⑰ 52 + 3 x 15
⑱ 15 x 53	⑲ 12 x 50 + 52 ÷ 4
⑳ $5\frac{1}{4} - 2\frac{1}{2}$	㉑ $\frac{7}{15} - \frac{1}{6}$
㉒ $3\frac{1}{4} + 1\frac{7}{8}$	㉓ 12.3 ÷ 100
㉔ Write $\frac{3}{4}$ as a %.	㉕ Which is bigger, $1\frac{3}{4}$ or $1\frac{2}{3}$?
㉖ Find the G.C.F. of 21 and 35.	㉗ Find the L.C.M. of 25 and 40.

Mrs. Saura goes shopping. Look at the map and help her solve the problems.

㉘ Use 24-h clock time to write the opening and closing times for the convenience stores.

㉙ How long is Ben's convenience store open every day? _____

㉚ How long is Lucy's convenience store open every day? _____

㉛ Mrs. Saura can cycle 55.8 m in 9 s. What is her speed? _____

㉜ Mrs. Saura cycles at a speed of 6 m/s. How long will it take her to go to Ben's convenience store? _____

㉝ How long will it take her to go to Lucy's convenience store? _____

㉞ Mrs. Saura leaves her home at 21:58:02. Which convenience store should she go to ? Why?

㉟ Mrs. Saura has 15 $20 bills and 12 $5 bills. How much does she have in all?

㊱ What fraction of Mrs. Saura's money is in $20 bills?

36

Look at the flyer. Answer Mrs. Saura's questions.

㊲ What fraction of the popsicles in the box are lemon flavoured? _____

㊳ What fraction of the popsicles in the box are blueberry flavoured? _____

㊵ What percent of the popsicles in the box are lime flavoured? _____

㊶ What percent of the popsicles in the box are strawberry flavoured? _____

㊸ What is the ratio of strawberry flavoured popsicles to the total number of popsicles in a box? _____

㊷ I bought 3 boxes of popsicles. I gave 9 lemon flavoured and 12 lime flavoured to my neighbours. How many popsicles do I have now? _____

㊸ How much do 5 boxes of popsicles cost? _____

㊹ How much does each roll of paper towel cost? _____

㊺ I have bought 7 toy cars. Each toy car needs 3 batteries to move. What is the minimum number of packs of batteries should I buy? _____

㊻ How much do I need to pay for 32 batteries? _____

㊼ I want 5 kg of ham and pay with 3 $20 bills. How much change will I get? _____

㊽ I cut the ham into slices. Each slice weighs 25 g. How many slices of ham will I get from 5 kg of ham? _____

Perimeter and Area

$$\begin{array}{r} 135 \\ 3.5 \\ \hline 1.0 \\ 4 \\ \hline 7.4 \end{array}$$

Determine the perimeter and area of each shape.

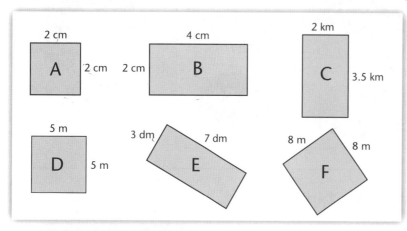

Quick Tip

Perimeter is the distance around the outside of a shape. It is measured in linear units, e.g. m, km.

Area is the space within a shape. It is measured in square units, e.g. cm^2, km^2.

Shape		A	B	C	D	E	F
①	Perimeter	8 cm	12 cm	11 km	20 m	20 dm	32 m
②	Area		cm^2	cm^2	km^2	m^2	dm^2	m^2

Find the perimeters (P) and areas (A) of the parallelograms. Show your work.

Example

Cut a right triangle from the left. Move it to the right to form a rectangle together with the unshaded part.

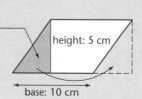

height: 5 cm

base: 10 cm

Area of parallelogram
= area of rectangle
= 5 x 10
= 50 cm^2

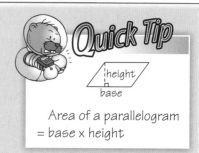

Quick Tip

height
base

Area of a parallelogram
= base x height

③

7 cm
5 cm
6 cm

P = ____2____ = __26__ cm
A = _____ = _____ cm^2

④

12 m
9 m
10 m

P = _____ = __240__ m
A = _____ = _____ m^2

⑤

60 cm
20 cm
25 cm

P = _____ = _____ cm
A = _____ = _____ cm^2

⑥

18 km
3 km
3.5 km

P = _____ = _____ km
A = _____ = _____ km^2

Find the perimeters (P) and areas (A) of the triangles. Show your work.

Example

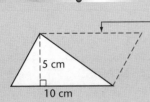

A parallelogram can be formed by 2 congruent triangles.

Area of a triangle $=$ half of the area of a parallelogram

Area of the triangle
= area of the parallelogram ÷ 2
= base x height ÷ 2
= 10 x 5 ÷ 2
= 25 cm^2

⑦

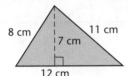

8 cm   11 cm
7 cm
12 cm

P = _____ = _____ cm

A = _____ = _____ cm^2

⑧

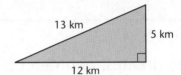

13 km   5 km
12 km

P = _____ = _____ km

A = _____ = _____ km^2

⑨

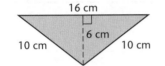

16 cm
6 cm
10 cm   10 cm

P = _____ = _____ cm

A = _____ = _____ cm^2

⑩

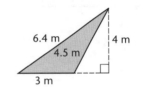

6.4 m   4 m
4.5 m
3 m

P = _____ = _____ m

A = _____ = _____ m^2

Draw 3 different parallelograms, each having an area of 12 cm^2.

1 cm
1 cm

⑪

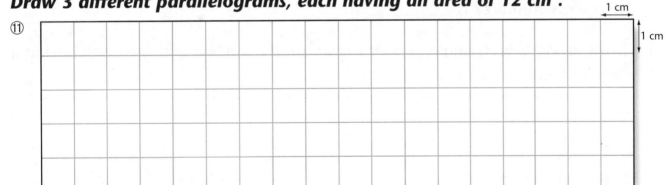

Draw 3 different triangles, each having an area of 10 cm^2.

1 cm
1 cm

⑫

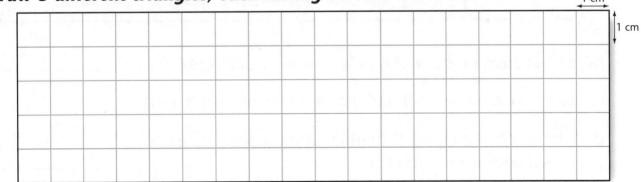

Draw the possible shapes. Label their dimensions and give the correct answers.

⑬ Draw 3 different rectangles, each having an area of 12 cm². Colour the rectangle which has the greatest perimeter.

a.

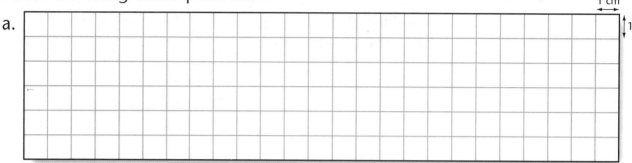

b. The greatest perimeter is _____ cm.

⑭ Draw 3 different rectangles, each having a perimeter of 18 m. Colour the rectangle which has the greatest area.

a.

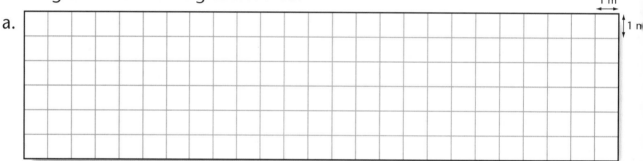

b. The greatest area is _____ m².

⑮ Draw an isosceles triangle, a right triangle and a scalene triangle, each having a base of 6 cm and a height of 4 cm.

a.

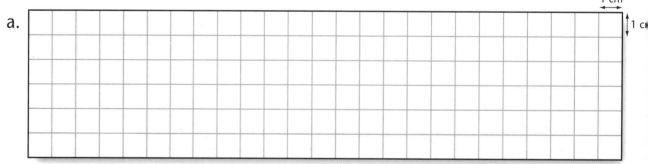

b. Are the areas of the triangles the same or different?   _____

c. Are the perimeters of the triangles the same or different?   _____

d. If the height and base of triangles are the same, are their areas the same or different?   _____

Solve the problems. Show your work.

⑯ A rectangular field measures 8.5 m by 6 m.

a. How many metres of fencing are needed to enclose the field?

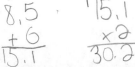

$$8.5$$
$$+6$$
$$\overline{15.1}$$

$$15.1$$
$$\times 2$$
$$\overline{30.2}$$

b. How many m² of turf must be laid to cover the whole field?

⑰ Sean has a poster with dimensions of 27 cm by 21 cm and a baseball card with dimensions of 9 cm by 7 cm. How many times is the poster larger than the card?

$$27$$
$$+21$$
$$\overline{48}$$

$$48$$ POSTER
$$\times 2$$
$$\overline{90}$$

$$9$$
$$+7$$
$$\overline{16}$$

$$16$$ BASEBALL
$$\times 2$$ CARD
$$\overline{32}$$

$$90$$
$$-32$$
$$\overline{58}$$ ← Larger

⑱ a. Calculate the area of the door.

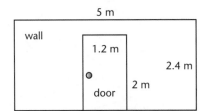

b. Calculate the area of the wall.

⑲ Antville is 13 km north of Beetown and Capeview is 20 km east of Beetown. What is the area enclosed by Antville, Beetown and Capeview?

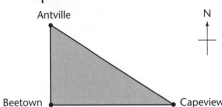

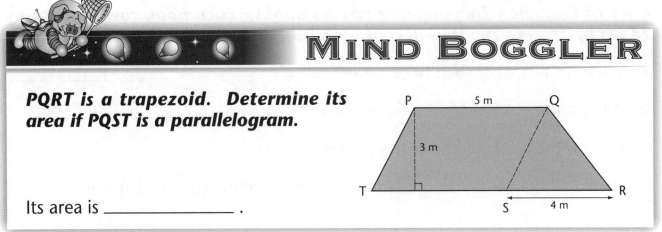

PQRT is a trapezoid. Determine its area if PQST is a parallelogram.

Its area is _____ .

9 Volume and Mass

84% 19   19½
22+2= 23   23

Example

Volume of a rectangular prism = Surface area of base x height

Volume = (22 x 12) x 10
= 2640 cm³

Volume = (12 x 10) x 22
= 2640 cm³

The volume remains the same no matter which surface is the base.

10 cm, 12 cm, 22 cm, base

22 cm, base, 12 cm, 10 cm

Find the volume of each of the following rectangular prisms.

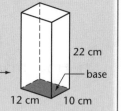

Quick Tip

height, base

Volume of a rectangular prism

= surface area of base x height

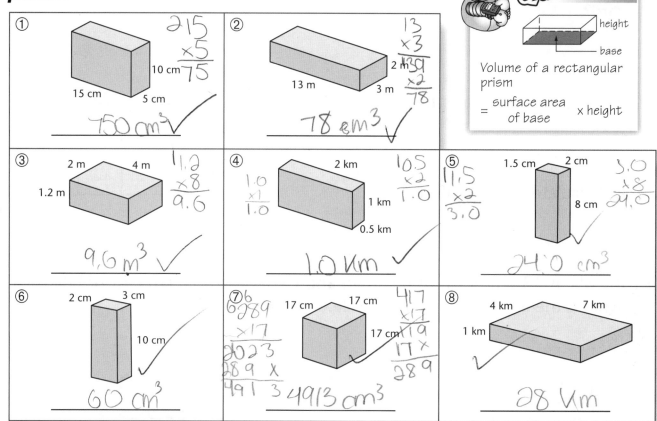

① 15 cm, 5 cm, 10 cm — 215 ×5 75 — 750 cm³ ✓

② 13 m, 3 m, 2 m — 13 ×3 39 ×2 78 — 78 cm³ ✓

③ 2 m, 4 m, 1.2 m — 11.2 ×8 9.6 — 9.6 m³ ✓

④ 2 km, 1 km, 0.5 km — 10.5 ×2 1.0, 1.0 ×1 1.0 — 1.0 km ✓

⑤ 1.5 cm, 2 cm, 8 cm — 11.5 ×2 3.0, 3.0 ×8 24.0 — 24.0 cm³

⑥ 2 cm, 3 cm, 10 cm — 60 cm³ ✓

⑦ 17 cm, 17 cm, 17 cm — 6289 ×17 ... 289 × 17 = 4913 — 4913 cm³

⑧ 4 km, 7 km, 1 km — 28 km

A set of Canadian Encyclopedia has 20 books. Each book cover measures 24 cm by 16 cm. The thickness of each book is 4 cm. Answer the questions.

⑨ What is the area of each book cover? — 1536 cm³ ___1536 cm³___

⑩ What is the volume of each book in cm³? — 1536 ×20 — ___1536 cm³___

⑪ What is the total volume of the 20 books in cm³? — 30720 — ___30,760 cm³___

⑫ Would all the books fit on a 1-m bookshelf of depth 20 cm? Explain.

No because 30,720 is over 1m and the depth is too small.

42

136
×3
108

0108
−84
24

21
×4
84

Sam and Jack use 1-cm³ blocks to build a tower having dimensions 7 cm by 4 cm by 3 cm. Check ✔ the tower they built and answer the questions.

⑬

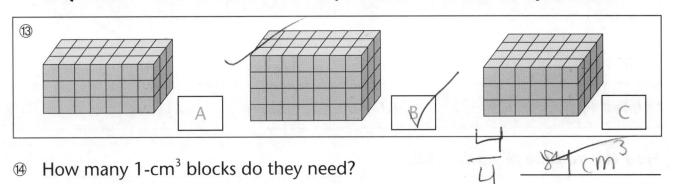

⑭ How many 1-cm³ blocks do they need? $\frac{4}{4}$ _84 cm³_

⑮ If they add more 1-cm³ blocks to build a new tower measuring 9 cm x 4 cm x 3 cm, how many additional blocks do they need?   _24_

Look at the following items in Ann's cupboard. Round all the dimensions to the nearest cm and use the rounded figures to find the volume of each item.

$\frac{4}{6}$

A

19 cm
Bran Flakes
25 cm
5.8 cm

⑯ Volume = _6_ x _19_ x _25_ = _2850_

⑰ Volume = _12_ x _12_ x _12_ = _1728_

B
12 cm
12 cm
12 cm

C
Butter
6 cm
12.2 cm   6 cm

⑱ Volume = _12_ x _6_ x _6_ = _432_

⑲ Volume = _5_ x _20_ x _6_ = _600_   100 x6   630

D
6 cm
Juice
20.5 cm
4.8 cm

E
22.3 cm
3 cm
Tea Bags
5 cm

⑳ Volume = _5_ x _3_ x _20_ = _300_

㉑ Volume = _4_ x _20_ x _15_ = _1200_   1384

F
15 cm
Cracker
22.8 cm
3.6 cm

㉒ List the items in order from the one with the smallest volume to the one with the largest. Write the letters only.

_F, E, C, D, B, A   x   E, C, D, F, B, A_ $\frac{1}{2}$

Fill in the missing information for each rectangular prism.

Volume (cm³)	㉓	㉔	147	16
Surface area of base (cm²)	25	12.5	㉕	320
Height (cm)	40	3	21	㉖

Find the volume of each solid.

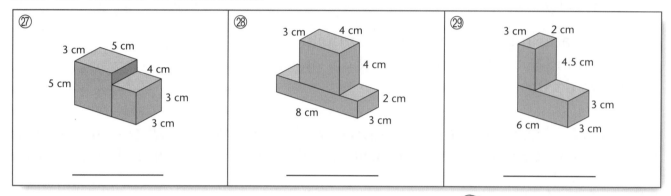

㉗ 5 cm, 3 cm, 5 cm, 4 cm, 3 cm, 3 cm, 3 cm

㉘ 3 cm, 4 cm, 4 cm, 2 cm, 8 cm, 3 cm

㉙ 3 cm, 2 cm, 4.5 cm, 3 cm, 6 cm, 3 cm

_____   _____   _____

Look at Tim's aquarium. Help Tim solve the problems. Show your work.

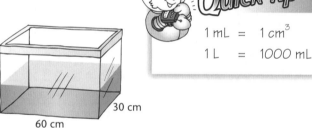

㉚ If the aquarium is filled to a depth of 15 cm, how many litres of water does it contain?

30 cm
60 cm

㉛ How many litres of water must be added if the depth of the water is increased to 16 cm?

㉜ If 18 litres of water is poured into the empty aquarium, what will the depth of the water be in the aquarium?

㉝ If the depth of the aquarium is 25 cm, what is the capacity of the aquarium in litres?

Kay is in a drugstore. Help her solve the problems.

Bottle weighs 40 g.
Each tablet weighs 500 mg.

Bottle weighs 50 g.
Each tablet weighs 500 mg.

Bottle weighs 35 g.
Each tablet weighs 250 mg.

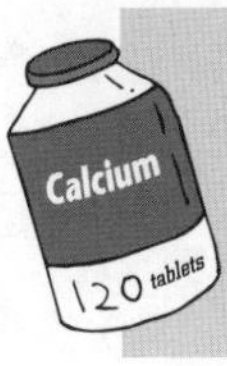

Bottle weighs 45 g.
Each tablet weighs 300 mg.

Quick Tip

1 kg = 1000 g
1 g = 1000 mg

㉞ What is the mass of a bottle of Vitamin C in g? ______________

㉟ What is the mass of a bottle of Vitamin E in g? ______________

㊱ What is the mass of a bottle of Aspirin in g? ______________

㊲ What is the mass of a bottle of calcium in g? ______________

㊳ There are 40 bottles of Vitamin C. How heavy are they in kg? ______________

㊴ There are 50 bottles of calcium. How heavy are they in kg? ______________

㊵ Kay's doctor recommends that she take about 1 g of calcium daily. How many tablets should she take daily? ______________

㊶ The pharmacist advises against taking more than 4 aspirin tablets daily. What is the maximum mass of aspirin Kay should take daily? ______________

MIND BOGGLER

The total mass of the calcium tablets in the bottle is 50 g. Answer the questions.

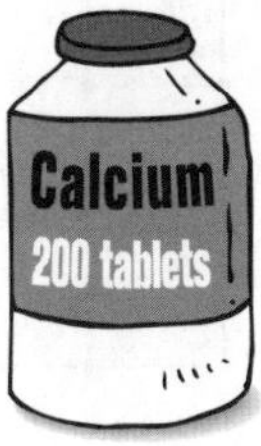

① What is the mass in g of each tablet? ______________

② If you take one tablet daily, how many grams of calcium will you take in May? ______________

10 Symmetry, 2-D and 3-D Figures

Draw all the lines of symmetry for each shape. Write the number of lines of symmetry in the circle.

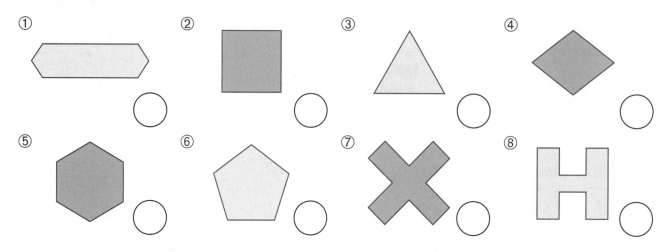

Use the lines of symmetry (dotted lines) to complete each shape.

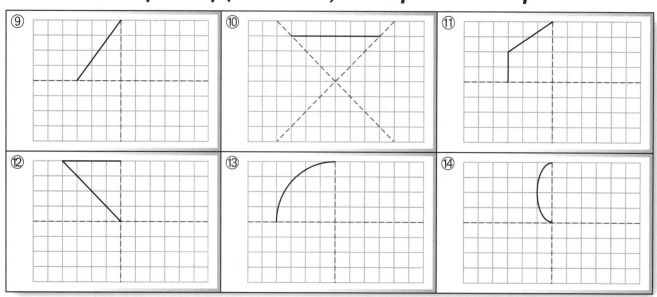

Add the minimum number of squares to each shape to make it symmetrical. Draw the square(s) and write the number.

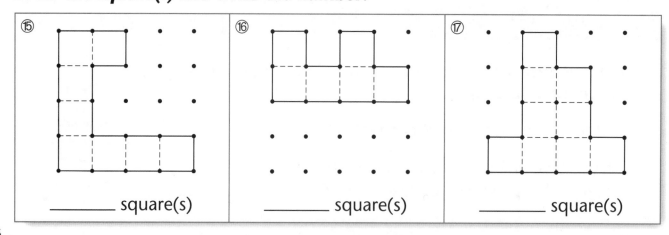

_____ square(s)   _____ square(s)   _____ square(s)

46

Write the order of rotational symmetry for the following shapes in the circles.

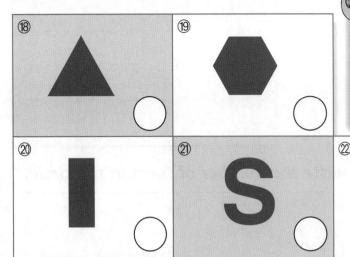

Quick Tip

A figure has rotational symmetry if it fits on itself within a complete rotation. The order of rotational symmetry is the number of times the figure fits on itself in one complete rotation,

e.g. ⅄ This figure has rotational symmetry of order 3.

⑱

⑲

⑳ **I**

㉑ **S**

㉒ **Z**

㉓

Use your protractor and ruler to construct the shapes.

㉔ Draw a triangle with only 1 line of symmetry.

㉕ Draw a right triangle with sides 3 cm, 4 cm and 5 cm.

㉖ Draw a triangle with angles 30°, 60° and 90°.

㉗ Draw a parallelogram with sides 3 cm and 5 cm, angles 60° and 120°.

㉘ Draw a rectangle with sides 12 cm and 2 cm. Then cut it into 8 identical triangles.

Draw one congruent and one similar figure for each shape.

㉙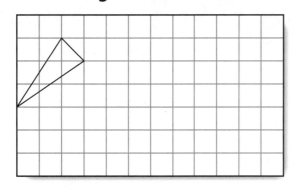

㉚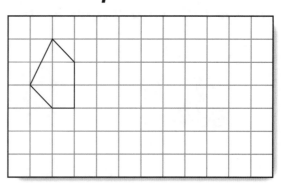

Complete the net for each solid and write the number of faces in the circle.

㉛ 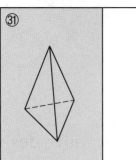 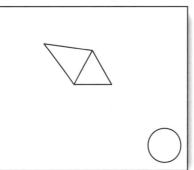 ○

㉜ 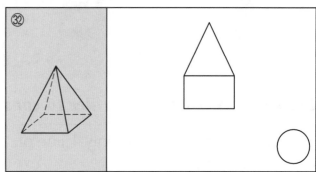 ○

㉝ 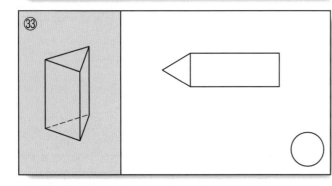 ○

㉞ 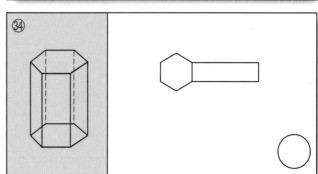 ○

Tom has built some models with interlocking cubes. Help him draw the models on the isometric dot paper.

㉟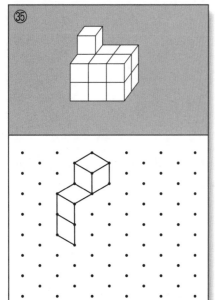

㊱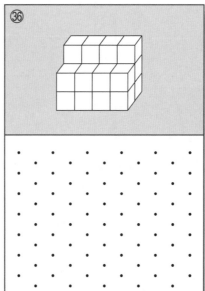

㊲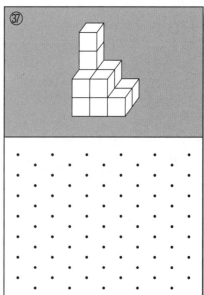

Write the names of the quadrilaterals.

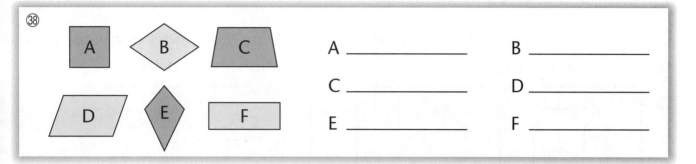

㊳

A _____ B _____

C _____ D _____

E _____ F _____

Check ✔ the boxes to show the properties of the shapes.

Property \ Quadrilateral	Rectangle	Rhombus	Parallelogram	Square
㊴ opposite sides parallel				
㊵ all sides equal				
㊶ 2 pairs of opposite sides equal				
㊷ all angles 90°				
㊸ 2 pairs of opposite angles equal				

Read the clues. Write the names of the geometric figures.

㊹ I am a solid with 6 congruent faces. _____

㊺ I am a solid with 4 faces. _____

㊻ I am a solid with 5 faces. _____

㊼ I am a 2-D figure with 4 lines of symmetry
and rotational symmetry of order 4. _____

MIND BOGGLER

Look at the views of the model and draw it out.

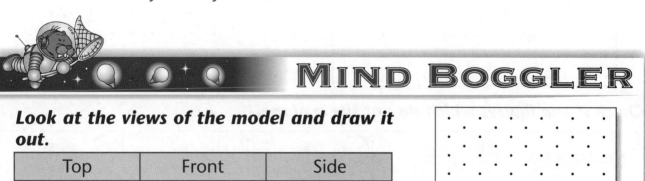

Top	Front	Side

11 Transformations and Coordinates

Each picture undergoes two transformations. Draw the images of the pictures.

① Reflection and rotation

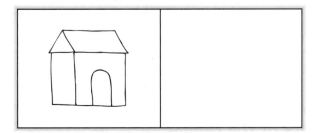

② Rotation and translation

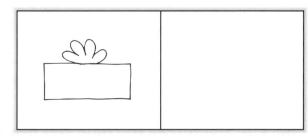

③ Reflection and translation

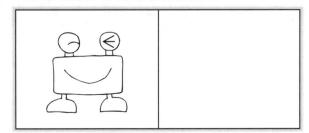

④ Rotation and reflection

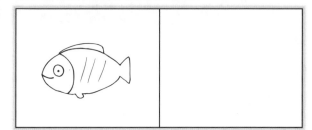

Complete the tiling using each shape.

⑤

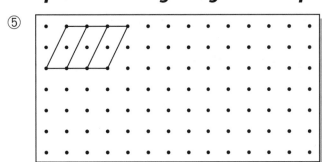

Quick Tip

Complete a tiling pattern using a shape by translating, reflecting or rotating the shape.

⑥

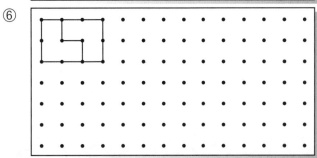

⑦

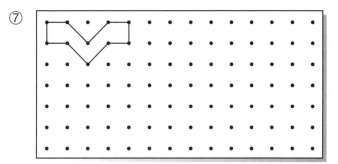

Check ✔ the figures which do not tile a plane.

⑧

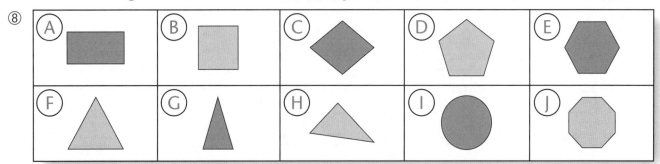

Draw the transformed images and answer the questions.

⑨ Reflect △ ABC in ℓ_1 and label it ★.

⑩ Reflect ★ in ℓ_2 and label it ♥.

⑪ Would the result be the same if you reflected △ ABC in ℓ_2 first and then ℓ_1?

_____

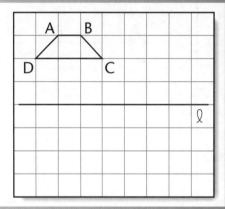

⑫ Translate trapezoid ABCD 3 units right and 1 unit down and label it ★.

⑬ Reflect ★ in ℓ and label it ♥.

⑭ Would the result be the same if you did the reflection before the translation?

_____

⑮ Reflect rectangle ABCD in ℓ and label it ★.

⑯ Rotate ★ a $\frac{1}{4}$ turn clockwise about point P and label it ♥.

⑰ Would the result be the same if you did the rotation before the reflection?

_____

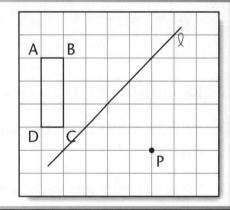

⑱ Rotate the shaded figure a $\frac{1}{4}$ turn clockwise about point P and label it ★.

⑲ Translate ★ 4 units down and 2 units left. Label it ♥.

⑳ What transformations could you do to the final image to get back to the original position?

_____

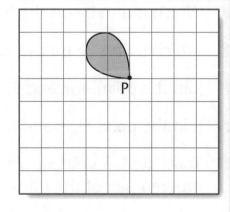

Write ordered pairs to represent each of the points plotted on the grid and answer the questions.

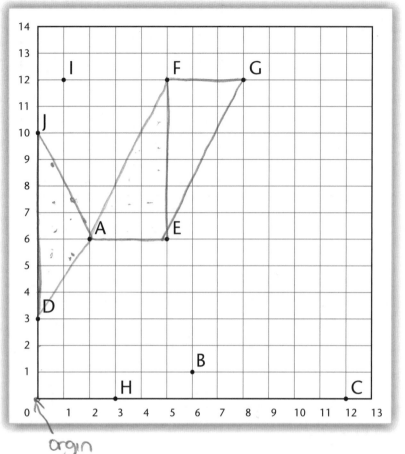

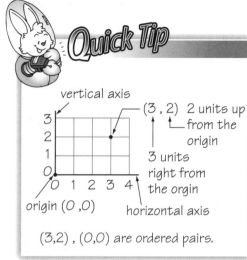

Quick Tip

vertical axis

(3 , 2) 2 units up
from the origin

3 units right from the origin

origin (0 ,0)

horizontal axis

(3,2) , (0,0) are ordered pairs.

㉑

A (_2_ , _6_) B (_1_ , _6_)

C (_0_ , _12_) D (_0_ , _3_)

E (_5_ , _6_) F (_5_ , _12_)

G (_8_ , _12_) H (_0_ , _3_)

I (_1_ , _12_) J (_0_ , _10_)

㉒ Join the points A, E, G and F. What shape is AEGF ? _Rhombus_

㉓ Which points have the same horizontal distance from the origin? _D, J_

㉔ Which points are vertically 12 units from the origin? _I, F, G_

㉕ Which points lie on the horizontal axis? _H, C_

㉖ Which points lie on the vertical axis? _D, J_

㉗ Join the point A, E and F. What is the area of △ AEF? _9_

㉘ Join the point D, A and J. What is the area of △ DAJ? _____

㉙ Translate E 3 units up and 2 units right. What is the ordered pair of the translated image? _____

㉚ How do you translate F to A? _____

㉛ How do you translate H to C? _____

52

Plot and join the points to see what shapes they are. Then label them and answer the questions.

- A (3 , 5) , B (2 , 2) , C (6 , 2)
- P (5 , 10) , Q (9 , 10) , R (9 , 6) , S (5 , 6)
- E (15 , 10) , F (19 , 10) , G (17 , 6) , H (13 , 6)
- L (11 , 5) , M (14 , 5) , N (14 , 0) , O (11 , 0)

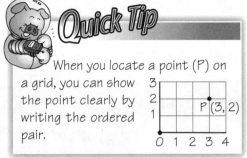

Quick Tip

When you locate a point (P) on a grid, you can show the point clearly by writing the ordered pair.

㉜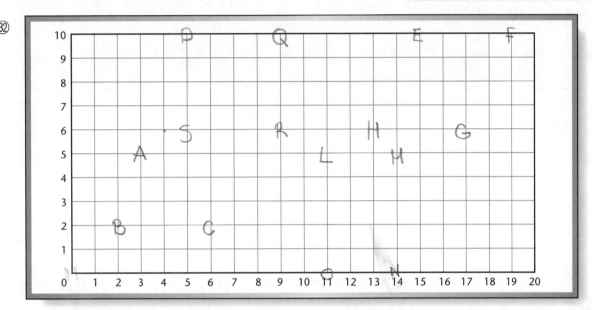

㉝ If A is moved 1 unit up and 1 unit right, what will its ordered pair be? After the translation, what kind of triangle is △ ABC?

Ordered pair = (4,6)

㉞ If H is moved 2 units right, what will its ordered pair be? After the translation, what shape is EFGH?

Ordered pair = (15-6)

MIND BOGGLER

What are the coordinates of point P?

If A (2, 8) is rotated $\frac{1}{2}$ turn about P, its image is at (4, 0).

The coordinates of point P are _____ .

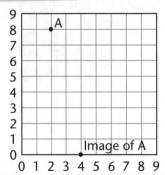

53

12 Patterns and Simple Equations

Sarah writes some patterns and asks Sunita to describe the rules and give the next 3 terms in each pattern. Help Sunita with her task.

Examples

① Continue the pattern 5 , 6 , 8 , 11 , ...
   5 , 6 , 8 , 11 , 15 , 20 , 25
      +1 +2 +3 +4 +5 +6

   Rule : The numbers increase by 1 more each time.

② Continue the pattern 4 , 9 , 19 , 39 , ...
   4 , 9 , 19 , 39 , 79 , 159
     4x2+1 9x2+1 19x2+1 39x2+1 79x2+1

   Rule : Double the previous term and add 1.

① 100 , 98 , 94 , 88 , _80_ , _70_ , _68_ , ...

   Rule : _The numbers decrease by 2,4,6 etc._

② 1 , 2 , 6 , 24 , ~~442~~ 120 , _120_ , _504~~0~~_ , ...

   Rule : _____

③ 50 , 48 , 51 , 49 , _52_ , _50_ , _53_ , ...

   Rule : _The numbers increase and decrease by adding 1._

④ 5 , 9 , 17 , 33 , _65_ , ____ , ____ , ...
        4 8 16
   Rule : _____

⑤ 1 , 4 , 9 , 16 , _25_ , _36_ , _49_ , ...

   Rule : _The numbers increase by 2 each time_

For each set of numbers, write the rule that relates the first two columns to the third. Then follow the rule to write another set of numbers in the boxes.

⑥

5	9	13
8	4	11
7	10	16
6	4	9

_____

⑦

18	3	7
20	4	6
15	5	4

_____

⑧

4	3	10
5	6	17
7	4	15

_____

The data in each table follow a pattern. Complete the tables and answer the questions.

⑨ Population of Markville

a.

Year	1980	1985	1990	1995	2000	2005
Population in thousands	69	77	89	105	125	149

8 12 16

b. In which year will the population be 177 000? _____

⑩ Cost of a movie ticket

a.

Year	1995	1996	1997	1998	1999	2000
Amount ($)	6.00	6.50	7.50	8.00	850	9.50

b. How much was a movie ticket in 2001? $10.00

⑪ Mass of a new born baby

a.

Age (month)	0	1	2	3	4	5	6
Mass (kg)	3.2	3.4	3.7	4.1	4.6	5.2	

2 3 4

b. When will the baby weigh 7.6 kg? _____

John saves money according to a pattern. Complete the graph to show the pattern and answer the questions.

⑫ a.

Money Saved by John

b. How much will he save by Week 12? $13.

c. After how many weeks will there be $20 in savings? $21

d. Describe John's saving pattern. Each week he adds a dollar.

The movement of gas price follows a pattern. Follow the pattern to complete the graph and answer the questions.

⑬ a.

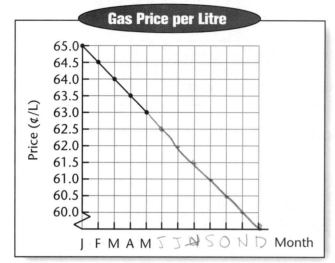

b. What will the gas price be in June?

   ~~162.50~~ 62.50

c. When will the gas price reach 60¢?

   November

Draw the next 2 diagrams in each pattern. Describe the changing rules for each figure.

⑭ a.

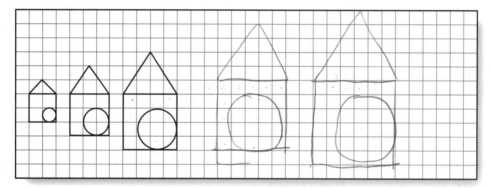

b. Triangle : It increased by

c. Square :

d. Circle :

⑮ a.

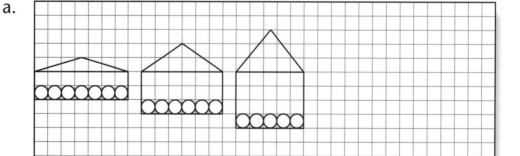

b. Triangle :

c. Rectangle :

d. Circle :

Read the number puzzles and find the numbers using the guess-and-test method.

⑯ Increase this number by 7 and then double it. The result is 70.

This number is ☐ .

⑰ The number is halved and then reduced by 20. The result is 30.

This number is ☐ .

⑱ Divide this number by 2 and then reduce it by 3. The result is 11.

This number is ☐ .

⑲ Add 25 to this number. Then multiply it by 3. The result is 120.

This number is ☐ .

⑳ This number is 7 more than half of 30.

This number is ☐ .

㉑ Half of this number is 7 more than 37.

This number is ☐ .

Determine the value of the missing number in each of the following equations.

㉒ _____ − 17 = 98

㉓ _____ + 23 = 170

㉔ 39 x _____ = 156

㉕ _____ x 13 = 117

㉖ 85 ÷ _____ = 17

㉗ _____ ÷ 12 = 8

㉘ 2 x _____ = 31 − 1

㉙ 5 x _____ = 8 + 92

㉚ 59 − 5 = _____ x 9

㉛ 30 − 9 = 2 _____ x 3

㉜ 520 ÷ 26 _____ = 13 + 7

㉝ 13 + _____ = 220 ÷ 11

Quick Tip

Do the part without missing terms first. Then 'guess and test' the missing numbers.

MIND BOGGLER

Stan uses toothpicks to make the following pattern. Complete the table and the statement.

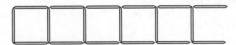

No. of squares	1	2	3	4	5	6	7	8
No. of toothpicks used	4	7	10					

To make 10 squares, Stan needs _____ toothpicks.

13 Data and Graphs

Choose the type of graph that best represents each of the following sets of data. Write the letters in the circles.

Quick Tip

Circle graph - To show the relationship between individual data and the whole data set
Bar graph   - To show the relationship between individual data pairs
Line graph   - To show the tendency of data to change

C - circle graph   B - bar graph   L - line graph

① Maximum daily temperature in Toronto each day in June — **L**

② Gas prices at different gas stations on a particular day — **B**

③ Percentage of money spent on different items (food, housing, etc) — **C**

④ Total number of goals scored by different hockey teams in a season — **L**

⑤ Changes in gas price over a 1-month period — **C**

⑥ Percentage of students with different Math grades (A to E) in a Grade 6 class — **B**

⑦ Number of students in a school with different hair colours — **C**

⑧ Changes in weight of Baby Sam during the first year — **L**

⑨ Comparison of masses of different types of dogs — **B**

⑩ Size of family among Grade 6 students — **B**

Melissa conducted a survey among 30 classmates in her Grade 6 class to find out their favourite snacks. Help her complete the tally chart and present the data in a bar graph and a circle graph.

⑪

Snack	Chips	Nuts	Chocolate	Candy	Ice cream
Tally	ⅢⅢ Ⅱ	ⅢⅢ	ⅢⅢ Ⅲ	Ⅲ Ⅰ	ⅢⅢ Ⅰ
No. of Students	7	5	8	4	6
Fraction of the Whole	$\frac{7}{30}$	$\frac{5}{30}$	$\frac{8}{30}$	$\frac{4}{30}$	$\frac{6}{30}$

⑫

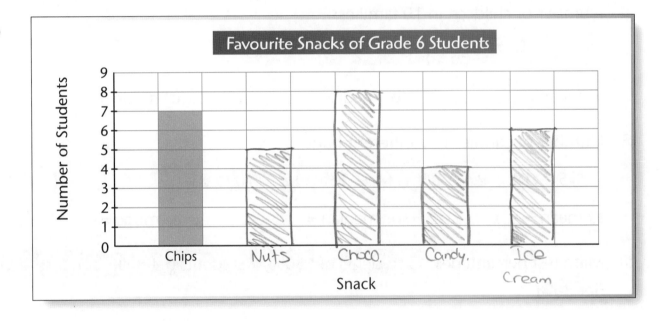

Favourite Snacks of Grade 6 Students

⑬

Favourite Snacks of Grade 6 Students

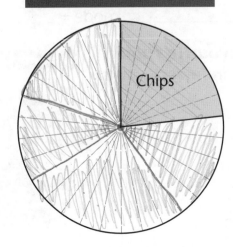

Quick Tip

Don't forget to label each axis in a bar graph and each sector in a circle graph.

59

Find the mean, median and mode of each set of data.

⑭ Gas price (¢/litre) over a 2-week period:

| 67.5 | 58.2 | 56.9 | 56.9 | 59.2 | 60.1 | 61.9 |

a. mean = _60.1_   b. median = _59.9_   c. mode = _56.9_

56.9 + 56.9 + 58.2 + 59.9 + 60.1 + 61.9 + 67.5 =
420.7 ÷ 7 =

⑮ Number of children in 10 families:

| 5 | 1 | 2 | 2 | 3 | 4 | 6 | 2 | 2 | 3 |

a. mean = _3_   b. median = _2.5_   c. mode = _2_

1 + 2 + 2 + 2 + 2 + 3 + 3 + 4 + 5 + 6 = 30

⑯ Number of candies in 9 different bags:

| 15 | 18 | 27 | 30 | 14 | 15 | 12 | 10 | 21 |

a. mean = _18_   b. median = _15_   c. mode = _15_

10 + 12 + 14 + 15 + 15 + 18 + 21 + 27 + 30 =
162 ÷ 9 = 18

⑰ Math test percentages: 3 students get 50%, 2 students get 60%, and 5 students get 80%

a. List the percentages of all 10 students in order from lowest to highest:

_50%, 50%, 50%, 60%, 60%, 80%, 80%, 80%, 80%, 80%_

b. mean : _67_   b. median = _70_   c. mode = _80_

50 + 50 + 50 + 60 + 60 + 80 + 80 + 80 + 80 + 80 = 670 ÷ 10 = 67

36 students were asked to choose their favourite colour. Look at the circle graph and write fractions in lowest terms to complete the statements below.

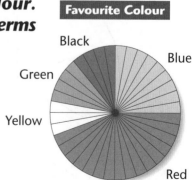

Favourite Colour

Black
Blue
Green
Yellow
Red

⑱ _____ of the students chose blue.

⑲ _____ of the students chose red.

⑳ _____ of the students did not choose blue.

Diane did a survey of the reading and TV watching habits of 15 friends. Look at the results and complete the table and the bar graph for each set of data. Answer the questions.

㉑

Reading Time (minutes / week)	20 25 60 30 40 50 55 80 100
	70 10 15 30 35 65

a.

Time in Minutes	Tally	No. of Students
1 - 20	|||	3
21 - 40	‖‖‖	5
41 - 60	|||	3
61 - 80	|||	3
81 -100	|	1

b.

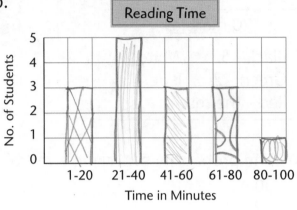

Reading Time

c. How many students read for more than 1 h a week? _____4_____

㉒

TV watching time (hours / week)	2 3 8 10 5 6 7 9 5 8 10
	9 2 1 5

a.

Time in Hours	Tally	No. of Students
1 - 2	|||	3
3 - 4	|	1
5 - 6	||||	4
7 - 8	|||	3
9 - 10	||||	4

b.

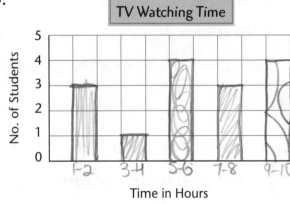

TV Watching Time

c. How many students watch TV for more than 6 h a week? _____7_____

MIND BOGGLER

Find 3 numbers which are all positive integers with a mean of 10 and a median of 8.

There are many possible answers.

The 3 numbers are __8, 8, 14__ .

14 Probability

Janice picks a marble from the box. Write the probability in fractions in lowest terms. Label each part of the circle graph to show the probability of picking marbles of different colours.

20 marbles

Black - 5   White - 4
Green - 2   Blue - 6
Red - the rest

Quick Tip

Probability = $\dfrac{\text{No. of times a particular event occurs}}{\text{No. of all possible events}}$

= fraction of times for a particular event to occur

Probability can also be written as a decimal or in %.

① The probability of picking a marble in

  a. black   _____

  b. blue   _____

  c. white   _____

  d. green   _____

  e. red   _____

  f. blue or red _____

② **Probability of Picking Marbles in Different Colours**

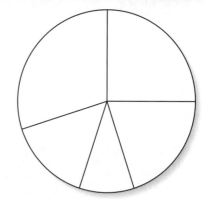

③ How can you increase the probability of picking a red marble?

_____

On a certain day in April the probability of rain is $\dfrac{3}{10}$, the probability of sun is $\dfrac{1}{5}$, the probability of mist is $\dfrac{1}{6}$ and the probability of cloud is $\dfrac{1}{3}$.

④ Is it more likely to be sunny or cloudy?   _____

⑤ Is it more likely to be rainy or sunny?   _____

⑥ What is the probability of not raining?   _____

⑦ List all the fractions representing the probabilities from least to greatest.

_____

⑧ List all the weather conditions from least likely to most likely.

_____

Sarah spins 2 identical spinners and multiplies the numbers that the arrows have landed on each time.

⑨ Complete the table to show all the possible outcomes.

X	1	2	3	4
1				
2				
3				
4				

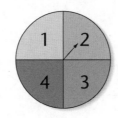 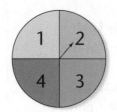

⑩ How many possible outcomes are there? _____

⑪ Which outcome is the most likely ? _____

⑫ What is the probability of getting the most likely outcome? _____

⑬ How many outcomes are greater than 10? _____

⑭ What is the probability of getting outcomes which are greater than 10? _____

⑮ What is the probability of getting outcomes which are not an even number? _____

Mr. and Mrs. Ling have 2 children. Complete the tree diagram to show all the possible combinations of boys (B) and girls (G). Then fill in the blanks.

⑯

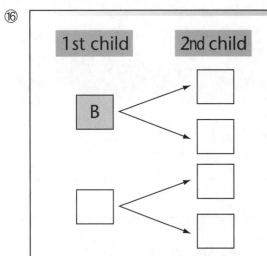

⑰ There are _____ combinations.

They are _____ .

⑱ The probability that the Lings have 2 girls is _____ .

⑲ The probability that they have 1 boy and 1 girl is _____ .

Look at the menu. Choose one item from each category and use a tree diagram to show all the possible combinations. Answer the questions.

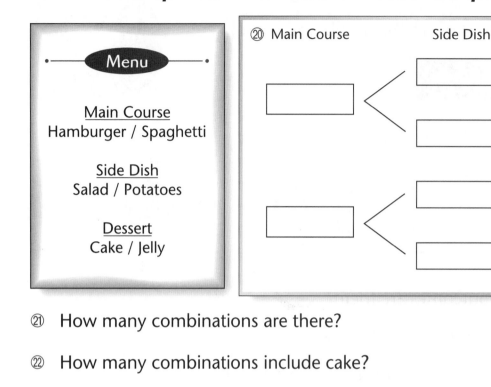

Menu

Main Course
Hamburger / Spaghetti

Side Dish
Salad / Potatoes

Dessert
Cake / Jelly

㉑ How many combinations are there? _____

㉒ How many combinations include cake? _____

㉓ How many combinations include salad? _____

㉔ How many combinations include hamburger and cake? _____

㉕ What is the probability of a customer choosing a meal with hamburger, salad and jelly? _____

㉖ What is the probability of a customer choosing a meal with hamburger, potatoes and cake? _____

Look at the food and drinks you can choose for tea time. Choose one item from each category and answer the questions.

Food   Sandwich (S)   Hot dog (H)
Doughnut (D)   Muffin (M)   Cookies (C)

Drinks   Coffee (CO)   Tea (T)

㉗ How many combinations are there? What are they?

_____

_____

㉘ What is the probability of getting a sandwich and coffee? _____

Sarah spins each spinner once to see what outfits she will put on. Draw a tree diagram to show all the combinations.

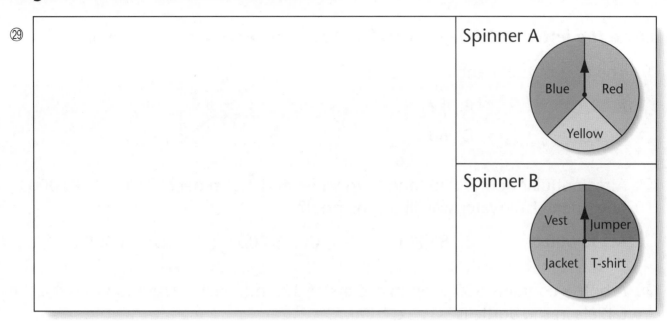

㉙

Spinner A

Spinner B

㉚ What is the probability that Sarah will put on a blue vest? _____

㉛ What is the probability that Sarah will put on yellow clothes? _____

㉜ What is the probability that she will put on a jumper? _____

㉝ Sarah changes the word 'Vest' in Spinner B to 'Jacket'.

   a. How many combinations will there be then? _____

   b. What kind of clothes is Sarah more likely to wear? _____

   c. What is the probability that Sarah will put on a blue jumper? _____

   d. What is the probability that she will put on a red jacket? _____

   e. What is the probability that she will put on a red or yellow T-shirt? _____

MIND BOGGLER

Jennifer has 3 hooks and 3 coats of different colours. If each hook holds only 1 coat, what is the probability that the red coat is on the 2nd hook?

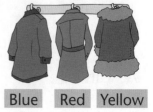

Blue   Red   Yellow

The probability is _____ .

Final Test

Circle the letter which represents the best answer to each question.

① The area of the triangle is _____ cm² .

   A. 6   B. 12

   C. 20   D. 60

   4 cm
   3 cm
   5 cm

② A rectangular pool is 5 m long, 2 m wide, and 1.5 m deep. If 1 m³ = 1000 L, how many L of water will fill up the pool?

   A. 30 000 L   B. 8500 L   C. 41 000 L   D. 15 000 L

③ A bottle contains 500 vitamin tablets of 325 mg each. The total mass of the tablets in the bottle is _____ g.

   A. 162.5   B. 1625   C. 16 250   D. 162 500

④ Which of the following letters has rotational symmetry of order 2?

   A. A   B. P   C. S   D. T

⑤ How many lines of symmetry does a parallelogram have?

   A. 0   B. 1   C. 2   D. 3

⑥ A net with 5 faces can be used to make a _____ .

   A. cube   B. rectangular   C. square   D. triangular
                       prism   pyramid   prism

⑦ A/An _____ triangle has 3 equal angles.

   A. right   B. equilateral   C. isosceles   D. scalene

⑧ 20 identical books fill a shelf of width 0.5 m. How thick is each book?

   A. 10 mm   B. 20 mm   C. 25 mm   D. 30 mm

⑨ Which of the following figures can tile a plane?

   A. Circles   B. Regular   C. Regular   D. Regular
                       pentagons   hexagons   octagons

⑩ The coordinates of point A are _____ .

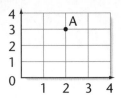

A. (3,4) B. (4,3)

C. (3,2) D. (2,3)

⑪ The translation of a point on a grid from (0,5) to (4,1) is 4 units _____ and 4 units _____ .

A. right, down B. right, up C. left, up D. left, down

⑫ The next 2 terms in the pattern 5, 1, 7, 2, ... are _____ .

A. 3, 9 B. 9, 3 C. 3, 4 D. 9, 8

⑬ Look at the changes in gas price.

Month	January	February	March	April
Gas price (¢/L)	68.2	68.0	67.6	67.0

If the trend continues, the gas price in June will be _____ ¢/L.

A. 65.2 B. 66 C. 66.2 D. 66.8

⑭ A number when doubled and then reduced by 2 gives 14. The number is _____ .

A. 4 B. 6 C. 8 D. 9

⑮ Join the points A, C and D. What kind of triangle do you get?

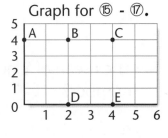

Graph for ⑮ - ⑰.

A. Right triangle B. Isosceles triangle

C. Equilateral triangle D. Scalene triangle

⑯ Which points are horizontally 2 units from the origin?

A. A and B B. B and C C. B and D D. C and E

⑰ What is the area of rectangle BCED?

A. 8 square units B. 6 square units C. 4 square units D. 10 square units

⑱ What fraction of a day does Dan spend at school?

Circle Graph for ⑱ - ⑳.

Dan's Daily Activities

School

Sleep

Other

Homework   TV

A. $\dfrac{1}{9}$ B. $\dfrac{1}{5}$

C. $\dfrac{1}{4}$ D. $\dfrac{1}{3}$

⑲ What fraction of a day does Dan spend on 'Other' activities?

A. $\dfrac{1}{2}$ B. $\dfrac{1}{4}$ C. $\dfrac{1}{8}$ D. $\dfrac{1}{10}$

⑳ What fraction of a day does Dan spend sleeping?

A. $\dfrac{1}{2}$ B. $\dfrac{1}{3}$ C. $\dfrac{1}{4}$ D. $\dfrac{1}{5}$

㉑ Find the median of 9, 5, 7, 11, 12.

A. 6   B. 7   C. 8.8   D. 9

㉒ Find the mean of 9, 16, 3, 9, 7.

A. 6   B. 7   C. 8.8   D. 9

㉓ Find the mode(s) of 5, 8, 2, 2, 8, 5, 5.

A. 2   B. 5   C. 2, 5   D. 2, 5, 8

㉔ The mean of 3 numbers is 10. Two of the numbers are 2 and 5. What is the 3rd number?

A. 3   B. 23   C. 17   D. 7

㉕ A family has 2 children. What is the probability that they are both girls?

A. $\dfrac{1}{2}$ B. $\dfrac{1}{3}$ C. $\dfrac{1}{4}$ D. $\dfrac{2}{3}$

㉖ A family has 3 children. What is the probability that all 3 children are boys?

A. $\dfrac{1}{9}$ B. $\dfrac{1}{8}$ C. $\dfrac{1}{4}$ D. $\dfrac{1}{3}$

Find the answers.

㉗ 324.9 ÷ 100 = ________

㉘ 0.0984 x 100 = ________

㉙ 5.982 x 3 = ________

㉚ 324.9 ÷ 3 = ________

㉛ 116 – 28 x 2 ÷ 7 = ________

㉜ 56 x 3 – 16 ÷ 4 = ________

㉝ 15 + 30 ÷ 6 = ________

㉞ 40 x 5 – 1 + 12 = ________

Complete the number sentences.

㉟ 15 x (7 – 2) = 15 x ______
= ______

㊱ 7 x (3 + 4) = 7 x 3 + 7 x ______
= ______

㊲ 7 + 9 x 2 = 7 + ______
= ______

㊳ (7 + 9) x 2 = ______ x ______
= ______

Write each number as a product of prime factors. Then determine the greatest common factor (G.C.F.) and the least common multiple (L.C.M.) of each pair of numbers.

㊴	a. 18 = ______________ 24 = ______________	b. G.C.F. of 18 and 24 : ________ L.C.M. of 18 and 24 : ________
㊵	a. 36 = ______________ 44 = ______________	b. G.C.F. of 36 and 44 : ________ L.C.M. of 36 and 44 : ________

Find the answers and write the fractions in lowest terms.

㊶ $\frac{2}{3} + \frac{3}{4}$ = ______

㊷ $\frac{7}{8} - \frac{3}{4}$ = ______

㊸ $1\frac{3}{5} - 1\frac{1}{4}$ = ______

㊹ $\frac{1}{6} + \frac{3}{8}$ = ______

㊺ $\frac{3}{4} - \frac{3}{8}$ = ______

㊻ $\frac{5}{6} - \frac{3}{4}$ = ______

㊼ $1\frac{3}{4} - 1\frac{1}{4}$ = ______

㊽ $\frac{1}{2} - \frac{1}{5}$ = ______

㊾ $2 - 1\frac{1}{8}$ = ______

㊿ $\frac{5}{4} - \frac{4}{5}$ = ______

(51) $\frac{2}{3} + \frac{5}{9}$ = ______

(52) $1\frac{4}{5} + \frac{5}{6}$ = ______

Find the volume of each solid. Then answer the question.

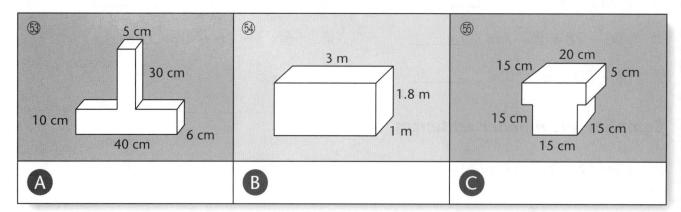

㊳ Which solid has the largest volume? _____

Draw all the lines of symmetry and write the order of rotational symmetry for each shape in the circle.

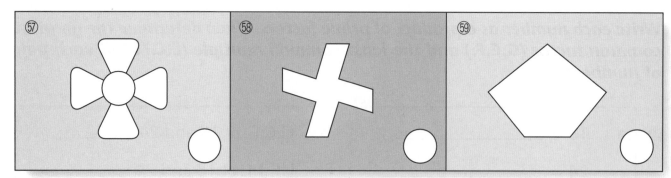

Find the next 3 terms for each pattern. Then write the rules.

㉀ 5, 9, 17, 33, 65, _____ , _____ , _____

Rule : _____

㉁ 500, 260, 140, 80, _____ , _____ , _____

Rule : _____

Determine the value of the missing numbers.

㉂ 25 ÷ _____ = 12.5   ㉃ _____ x 4 = 108   ㉄ 26.5 – _____ = 14

㉅ 15 + _____ = 20.3   ㉆ _____ ÷ 5 = 52.5   ㉇ 14 x 6 – _____ = 28

Sami eats $\frac{3}{4}$ *of a chocolate bar. Fred eats* $\frac{2}{3}$ *of a chocolate bar, and Steve eats* $\frac{3}{2}$ *of a chocolate bar. Help them solve the problems.*

⑥⑧　Who eats the most?　　　　　　　　　　　_____

⑥⑨　Who eats the least?　　　　　　　　　　　_____

⑦⓪　How many chocolate bars do they eat altogether?　　_____ bars

⑦①　If they have 4 chocolate bars, how much is left over?　_____ bars

⑦②　Each chocolate bar costs $0.98. If they want to buy
　　　4 chocolate bars, how much change do they get
　　　from $5?　　　　　　　　　　　　　　　_____

⑦③　If each chocolate bar weighs 225 g, how many
　　　kilograms do 50 chocolate bars weigh?　　　_____

Mary is cycling from Georgetown to Rosehill via Huttonville. She records her times at each location using a digital watch. Help her solve the problems.

⑦④　How long does Mary take to cycle from Georgetown
　　　to Huttonville?　　　　　　　　　　　　_____ min

⑦⑤　How long does Mary take to cycle from Huttonville to
　　　Rosehill?　　　　　　　　　　　　　　　_____ min

⑦⑥　What is her speed from Georgetown to Huttonville?　_____ km/h

⑦⑦　What is her speed from Huttonville to Rosehill?　　_____ km/h

⑦⑧　What is her average speed over the whole journey from
　　　Georgetown to Rosehill?　　　　　　　　　_____ km/h

A teacher measures the heights of 20 students in cm. Complete the table and the graphs using the data. Then answer the questions.

| 152 | 158 | 165 | 169 | 172 | 174 | 175 | 180 | 175 | 162 |
| 165 | 162 | 168 | 175 | 176 | 152 | 160 | 165 | 158 | 162 |

79

Range of Height (cm)	Tally	No. of Students	Fraction of the Whole
150 - 159			
160 - 169			
170 - 179			
180 - 189			

80

Height of Students

81

Height of Students

9
8
7
6
5
4
3
2
1
0

82 A student is picked by the teacher to clean the blackboard. What is the probability that a student between 150 cm and 159 cm is picked ? _____

83 What is the most likely height range among the students? _____

84 There are 5 girls between 170 cm and 179 cm. The teacher wants to pick a student between 170 cm and 179 cm. What is the probability that the teacher will pick a girl? _____

85 Use your calculator to find the mean height of the students. Write your answer to the nearest tenth. _____

Review

1. 1.05
2. 9800
3. 32.58
4. 413 ; 1180 ; 1593
5.
```
      8 2 0
  9 ) 7 3 8 0
      7 2
      ----
        1 8
        1 8
        ----
```
6.
```
        6.4 8
  5 ) 3 2.4
      3 0
      ----
        2 4
        2 0
        ----
          4 0
          4 0
          ----
```
7. 103
8. 5900
9. 1200
10. 10.2
11. 1
12. 8.01
13. ✔ ; 591 x 5 = 2955
14. 564 x 7 = 3948
15. ✔ ; 398 x 6 + 2 = 2390
16. ✔ ; 50 x 80 = 4000
17. ✔ ; 4000 ÷ 10 = 400
18. 50 x 40 = 2000
19. a. 0.29   b. 1.35   c. $\frac{5}{10}$ d. $\frac{8}{100}$ e. $1\frac{13}{100}$
20. a. $2\frac{1}{3}$ b. $4\frac{3}{7}$ c. $\frac{5}{4}$ d. $\frac{22}{5}$ e. $\frac{31}{8}$
21. 16 ; 22 ; 29
22. 64 ; 128 ; 256
23. 10 ; 12 ; 13
24. 65 ; 55 ; 50
25. 10 ; 14
26. 9 ; 12
27. 10.8 ; 15.6
28. 200
29. 50
30. 100
31. 10
32. 105
33. 55
34. $\frac{1}{4}$
35. 324
36. (Suggested answers) 12 , 27 ; 6 , 54 ; 4 , 81 ; 3 , 108
37. 150
38.
39. ✔
40. ✔
41.
42. ✔
43. ✔
44. A (3 , 2) B (3 , 4) C (5 , 2) D (4 , 0) E (0 , 5) F (6 , 4)
45. triangle
46. A ; B ; C ; E
47.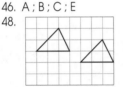
48.
49.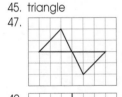
50. Rotation
51. Reflection
52. Translation
53. Reflection
54. 150
55. 250

1 Operations with Whole Numbers

1. 11 157
2. 8119
3. 9065
4. 56 119
5. 43 652
6.
```
      5 2 3
  x    1 4
  --------
    2 0 9 2
    5 2 3 0
  --------
    7 3 2 2
```
7.
```
      2 7 8
  x    3 6
  --------
    1 6 6 8
    8 3 4 0
  --------
  1 0 0 0 8
```
8.
```
        9 0 1
  x      4 9
  ----------
      8 1 0 9
    3 6 0 4 0
  ----------
    4 4 1 4 9
```
9.
```
      6 4 5
  x    2 8
  --------
    5 1 6 0
  1 2 9 0 0
  --------
  1 8 0 6 0
```
10.
```
        4 6
  13 ) 5 9 8
        5 2
        ----
          7 8
          7 8
          ----
```
11.
```
        1 8 2
  27 ) 4 9 1 4
        2 7
        ----
        2 2 1
        2 1 6
        ----
            5 4
            5 4
            ----
```
12.
```
        3 9 R4
  36 ) 1 4 0 8
        1 0 8
        ----
          3 2 8
          3 2 4
          ----
              4
```
13.
```
        4 5 4 R6
  13 ) 5 9 0 8
        5 2
        ----
          7 0
          6 5
          ----
            5 8
            5 2
            ----
              6
```
14. 2000 ; 1000 ; 3000 ; 6000 ; 6487

15. 6000 ; 2000 ; 1000 ; 9000 ; 9188
16. 12 000 ; 1000 ; 11 000 ; 11 217
17. 17 000 ; 5000 ; 12 000 ; 12 129
18. 9481 ; 20 ; 500 ; 10 000
19. 4368 ; 200 ; 20 ; 4000
20. 16 128 ; 400 ; 40 ; 16 000
21. 115 ; 6000 ; 50 ; 120
22. 157 R 5; 3000 ; 20 ; 150
23. 108 R 22 ; 4000 ; 40 ; 100
24. C ; E ; F ; G ; H
25. 24 ; 119
26. 17 ; 46
27. 300 + 34 ; 334
28. 512 – 4 ; 508
29. 7 + 360 ; 367
30. Ming has: 12 x 25 + 15 x 10 + 13 x 5 = 515 ; 515
31. Susanna has: 108 x 25 = 2700 ; 2700
32. No. of dimes: 56 x 25 ÷ 10 = 140 ; 140
33. Difference in amount: 458 x 25 – 192 x 10 = 9530 ; 9530
34. No. of chocolate eggs : 365 x 12 = 4380
    He eats 4380 chocolate eggs.
35. No. of small boxes : 4380 ÷ 50 = 87R30
    Keith will eat about 87 small boxes of chocolate.
36. No. of chocolate eggs : 58 x 3 + 96 x 2 = 366
    He has 366 chocolate eggs in all.
37. Dave's guess is the closest, only 8 more than the actual amount.
38. No. of chocolate eggs : 2858 ÷ 30 = 95R8
    Each bag contains about 95 chocolate eggs.

Mind Boggler

148

2 Decimals

1. 200 + 50 + 7 + 0.1 + 0.02 + 0.008 ; Two hundred fifty-seven and one hundred twenty-eight thousandths
2. 300 + 50 + 1 + 0.08 + 0.002 ; Three hundred fifty-one and eighty-two thousandths
3. 5406.903
4. 620.58
5. 59.01 < 59.05 < 59.1 < 59.15
6. 15.224 < 15.238 < 15.304 < 15.322
7.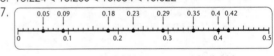
8. 0.004
9. 0.008
10. 0.012
11. 0.021
12. 0.026
13. 0.045
14. 50.05
15. 6.16
16. 11.87
17. 11.13
18. 1.406
19. 4.172
20. 0.306
21. 14.505
22. 2936
23. 5873
24. 1390.5
25. 91 640
26. 25 110
27. 402.3
28. 2 ; 1080
29. 9 ; 765
30. 2.35 x 100 x 8 ; 1880
31. 12.4 x 10 x 6 ; 744
32. 569.43
33. 27.18
34. 1623.78
35. 650.36
36. 2500.46
37. 2292.227
38. 365.048
39. 265.92
40. 5.823
41. 2.513
42. 2.465
43. 4.25
44. 28.59
45. 23.94
46.
```
        3.8 7
  6 ) 2 3.2 2
      1 8
      ----
        5 2
        4 8
        ----
          4 2
          4 2
          ----
```
47.
```
        4 7.5
  9 ) 4 2 7.5
      3 6
      ----
        6 7
        6 3
        ----
          4 5
          4 5
          ----
```

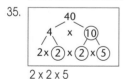

48. 7 ⟌ 211.26 = 30.18

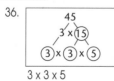

49. 8 ⟌ 96.64 = 12.08

50. 1.154	51. 7.482	52. 7.523
53. 6.88	54. 4.087	55. 19.253
56. ✗	57. ✔	58. ✗
59. ✗	60. ✔	61. ✔
62. 0.65	63. 1.485	64. 26.04
65. 9.96	66. 1.07	

67. 2.49 – 0.25 x 9 = 0.24 ; She needs to pay $0.24 more.
68. 4.34 x 3 + 3.24 x 2 = 19.50 ; She needs to pay $19.50.
69. 0.495 ÷ 3 = 0.165 ; There is 0.165 kg of shredded wheat in each portion.

Mind Boggler

1.127

3 Integers and Number Theory

1. A –3 ; B –2 ; C 0 ; D 5
2. 3   3. –3   4. 2   5. 0
6. 1   7. –2   8. 0   9. 4
10. –3°C ; –2°C ; 4°C ; 3°C ; 0°C ; 2°C ; –1°C
11. Sunday   12. Tuesday
13. 3   14. Thursday
15.-17.

18. 5 ; 20 and 40   19. 6 ; 12, 24, 36 and 48
20. 20   21. 12
22. 3, 6, 9, 12, 15, 18, 21, 24, 27, 30
23. 5, 10, 15, 20, 25, 30, 35, 40, 45, 50
24. 8, 16, 24, 32, 40, 48, 56, 64, 72, 80
25. 10, 20, 30, 40, 50, 60, 70, 80, 90, 100
26. 15, 30, 45 ; 24, 48, 72 ; 40, 80, 120 ; 10, 20, 30
27. 15 ; 24 ; 40 ; 10   28. 12 ; 6 ; 4 ; 1, 2, 3, 4, 6, 12
29. 20 ; 10 ; 5 ; 1, 2, 4, 5, 10, 20
30. 1, 2, 4 ; 4
31. 1, 2, 4, 8, 16 ; 1, 2, 3, 6, 9, 18 ; 1, 2 ; 2
32. 1, 3, 5, 15 ; 1, 2, 3, 5, 6, 10, 15, 30 ; 1, 3, 5, 15 ; 15
33. 1, 2, 5, 10 ; 1, 2, 3, 4, 6, 8, 12, 24 ; 1, 2 ; 2
34.

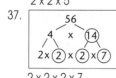

35.

40 = 4 x 10 = 2 x 2 x 2 x 5

2 x 2 x 5

36.

45 = 3 x 15 = 3 x 3 x 5

3 x 3 x 5

37.

56 = 4 x 14 = 2 x 2 x 2 x 7

2 x 2 x 2 x 7

38. 2 x 2 x 2 x 3 x 3   39. 2 x 2 x 2 x 2 x 2

40. 2 x 2 x 3 x 5   41. 2 x 5 x 5
42. 2 x 3 x 3 x 3   43. 2 x 2 x 2 x 2 x 5
44. 3 x 7 ; 2 x 2 x 7 ; 7 ; 84
45. 2 x 2 x 2 x 2 ; 2 x 2 x 2 x 3 ; 8 ; 48
46. 3 ; 4 ; 21 ; 28 ; 49   47. 7 ; 2 ; 84 ; 24 ; 60
48. 20 ; 7 ; 180 ; 63 ; 243   49. 50 ; 1 ; 400 ; 8 ; 392
50. 2 ; 100 ; 2 ; 500 ; 10 ; 490

Mind Boggler

1. 34 ; even   2. 12 ; even   3. 25 ; odd

4 Percent

1. 69%	2. 100%	3. 8%
4. 26%	5. 42%	6. 7%
7. 83%	8. 98%	9. 32%
10. 8%	11. 55%	12. 78%

13. 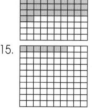 14.

15. 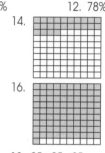 16.

17. 15 ; 15 ; 15   18. 25 ; 25 ; 25
19. 60 ; 60 ; 60   20. 30 ; 60 ; 80
21. 25 ; 50 ; 75   22. 86 ; 86
23. 85 ; 85   24. 90 ; 90
25. 65 ; 65   26. 92 ; 92
27. 85 ; 85   28. $\frac{1}{5}$

29. $\frac{1}{4}$ 30. $\frac{1}{2}$ 31. $\frac{3}{4}$

32. $\frac{41}{50}$ 33. $\frac{2}{25}$ 34. $\frac{4}{25}$

35. $\frac{33}{100}$ 36. 2   37. 0.26

38. 0.37   39. 0.95   40. 0.66

41. 0.09   42. 0.74   43. $\frac{1}{8}$

44. $\frac{19}{25}$ 45. $\frac{7}{10}$ 46. $\frac{9}{20}$

47. 0.7 ; $\frac{7}{100}$; $\frac{7}{10}$ 48. 60% ; $\frac{60}{100}$; $\frac{3}{5}$

49. 45% ; 0.45 ; $\frac{9}{20}$ 50. 5% ; 0.05 ; $\frac{5}{100}$

51. 26%   52. 78%
53. 86%   54. 52%
55. 11%   56. 7%

57. 0.27 ; $\frac{19}{50}$; 59%   58. 64% ; $\frac{18}{25}$; 0.93

59. 71% ; 0.73 ; $\frac{3}{4}$ 60. 75 ; 75

60. 35 ; 35   61. 35 ; 35
62. 186 ; 186   63. 11 ; 11
64. a. 43%   b. 27%   c. 30%   d. 38%   e. 62%
65. a. 20%   b. 80%   c. 50%   d. 40%
66. Tim eats: $\frac{18}{30} = \frac{6}{10} = \frac{60}{100} = 60\%$

Ray eats : $\frac{16}{25} = \frac{64}{100} = 64\%$

Tim eats 60% and Ray eats 64%. Ray's percent is higher.

Mind Boggler

If there are same numbers of marble in each colour,

there should be 25 marbles in each colour. Then each colour should make up 25% instead of 26% of the marbles.

5 Fractions

1. $1\frac{1}{2}$ 2. $1\frac{4}{5}$ 3. $2\frac{5}{6}$

4. $2\frac{1}{6}$ 5. $1\frac{1}{4}$ 6. $6\frac{1}{2}$

7. $1\frac{11}{18}$ 8. $2\frac{1}{5}$ 9. $2\frac{1}{3}$

10. $1\frac{1}{6}$ 11. $1\frac{7}{18}$ 12. $1\frac{5}{18}$

13. PRACTICE MAKES PERFECT

14. $\frac{4}{8} < \frac{5}{8} < \frac{7}{8}$ 15. $\frac{9}{10} < \frac{9}{7} < \frac{9}{4}$

16. $2\frac{3}{5} < 2\frac{4}{5} < 3\frac{1}{5}$ 17. $1\frac{1}{6} < 1\frac{5}{6} < 2\frac{5}{6}$

18. $\frac{5}{2}$ 19. $\frac{8}{5}$ 20. $\frac{13}{12}$

21. $\frac{13}{4}$ 22. $\frac{15}{6}$ 23. $\frac{12}{5}$

24. $\frac{16}{6}$ 25. $\frac{17}{4}$ 26. $\frac{16}{7}$

27. $\frac{2}{6}; \frac{3}{6}; \frac{5}{6}$ 28. $\frac{4}{9}; \frac{2}{9}; \frac{6}{9}; \frac{2}{3}$

29. $\frac{5}{8}; \frac{4}{8}; \frac{1}{8}$ 30. $\frac{5}{6}; \frac{2}{6}; \frac{3}{6}; \frac{1}{2}$

31. $\frac{6}{18}; \frac{1}{3}$ 32. $\frac{14}{20}; \frac{7}{10}$ 33. $\frac{30}{30}; 1$

34. $\frac{6}{15}; \frac{2}{5}$ 35. $\frac{20}{25}; \frac{4}{5}$ 36. $\frac{12}{42}; \frac{2}{7}$

37. $\frac{2}{12}; \frac{1}{6}$ 38. $\frac{1}{6}; \frac{1}{2}; \frac{1}{6}; \frac{3}{6}; \frac{4}{6}; \frac{2}{3}$

39. $\frac{6}{8}; \frac{1}{2}; \frac{6}{8}; \frac{4}{8}; \frac{2}{8}; \frac{1}{4}$

40. $2; 3; \frac{1}{2}$ 41. $5; 4; \frac{2}{5}$

42. $7; 14; 9; 1\frac{1}{8}$ 43. $5; 20; 27; 2\frac{1}{4}$

44. $\frac{3}{6} + \frac{2}{6} = \frac{5}{6}$ 45. $\frac{9}{15} - \frac{5}{15} = \frac{4}{15}$

46. $\frac{7}{3} - \frac{7}{15} = \frac{35}{15} - \frac{7}{15} = 1\frac{13}{15}$

47. $\frac{23}{6} - \frac{5}{4} = \frac{46}{12} - \frac{15}{12} = 2\frac{7}{12}$

48. $\frac{7}{5} + \frac{21}{10} = \frac{14}{10} + \frac{21}{10} = 3\frac{1}{2}$

49. $\frac{15}{8} + \frac{11}{4} = \frac{15}{8} + \frac{22}{8} = 4\frac{5}{8}$

50. $\frac{7}{4} - \frac{5}{8} = \frac{14}{8} - \frac{5}{8} = 1\frac{1}{8}$

51. $\frac{10}{3} - \frac{9}{4} = \frac{40}{12} - \frac{27}{12} = 1\frac{1}{12}$

52. $2\frac{1}{4}$ 53. 4 54. $\frac{1}{2}$

55. $2\frac{3}{10}$ 56. $1\frac{11}{12}$ 57. $2\frac{1}{12}$

58. $5\frac{1}{4}$ 59. $3\frac{3}{8}$ 60. $1\frac{7}{8}$

61. $\frac{2}{3}$

Mind Boggler

1

6 Rate and Ratio

1. 2.5   2. 20   3. 60
4. 6   5. 3   6. 4
7. 2.5   8. 14   9. 0.40
10. 1.20   11. 4.27

12. 6.60 ; 6.45 ; 6.85 ; B   13. 1.19 ; 1.25 ; 1.42 ; A
14. 0.79 ; 0.68 ; 0.89 ; B
15.-18. (Suggested answers)
15. 10 : 14 ; 15 : 21   16. 8 : 18 ; 12 : 27
17. 2 : 3 ; 20 : 30   18. 3 : 5 ; 6 : 10
19. 3 : 1   20. 1 : 4   21. 17 : 3
22. 7 : 18   23. 2 : 3   24. 6 : 5
25. 5 : 4   26. 2 : 3   27. 1 : 3
28. 2 : 5   29. $\frac{9}{25}$; 0.36 ; 36%

30. 2 : 5 ; 0.4 ; 40%   31. 41 : 50 ; $\frac{41}{50}$; 82%

32. 13 : 20 ; $\frac{13}{20}$; 0.65   33. 3 : 20 ; $\frac{3}{20}$; 15%

34. 2 : 1   35. 2 : 3   36. 5 : 9
37. 1 : 3   38. 2 : 3   39. 2 : 5
40. 3 : 5   41. 1 : 3   42. 2 : 3
43. $1.62   44. $6.48   45. 48¢
46. 15 stickers   47. 23 : 22   48. 15 stickers/day
49. a. 2 : 1   b. 1 : 3   c. 0.5 balloon/min
50. a. 5 : 2   b. 35 cards/year   c. 175 cards
    d. 49 cards/year   e. 49 0 cards

Mind Boggler

1. $2400/month   2. $900
3. $600   4. 1 : 2

7 Time, Distance and Speed

1. 16:35   2. 06:12   3. 11:25:46
4. 22:42:11   5. 16:27:53
6.    7.

5:35:10 p.m.   5:32:02 a.m.
8.    9.

12:05:33 p.m.   9:16:45 p.m.
10. 11:11:20   11. 07:31:05   12. 13:37:50
13. 2 h 10 min 35 s   14. 8 h 44 min 43 s   15. 120
16. 5   17. 800   18. 9
19. 4000   20. 2.5   21. 840
22. 0.66   23. 2.5   24. 7.5
25. 37.2   26. 4.52   27. 28 m
28. 30 cm   29. 9 mm   30. 560 km
31. 3000   32. 2   33. 0.6
34. 1.5   35. 4.4   36. 4
37. The shortest distance is to pass through the community centre and the museum. The distance is 5.4 km.
38. 25 km/h   39. 64 km/h   40. 2.5 m/s
41. 92 km   42. 70 km   43. 2 s
44. 25 s   45. 80 km/h   46. 10 h
47. 11.5 km/h   48. 51.75 km   49. 7 h
50. Paul's speed : 7 km in $\frac{1}{2}$ h → 14 km in 1 h ;
    Pat's speed : 24 km in 2 h → 12 km in 1 h ; Paul
51. a. 10:20:50 ; 10:20:55 ; 10:21:00 ; 10:21:04 ; 10:21:05
    b. 12:11:45 ; 12:12:15 ; 12:12:30 ; 12:12:40 ; 12:12:55

52. 15 s
53. 1 h 45 min 10 s
54. 36 s
55. 540 s or 9 min
56. 100 m
57. 2 m/s
58. 120 m

Mind Boggler

2000

Progress Test

1. C
2. D
3. A
4. A
5. B
6. B
7. C
8. D
9. B
10. B
11. D
12.
$$\begin{array}{r} 123 \\ \times\ 47 \\ \hline 4920 \\ 861 \\ \hline 5781 \end{array}$$

13. 2400.65

14.
$$\begin{array}{r} 54 \\ 29\overline{)1566} \\ 145 \\ \hline 116 \\ 116 \\ \hline \end{array}$$

15.
$$\begin{array}{r} 8.64 \\ 3\overline{)25.92} \\ 24 \\ \hline 19 \\ 18 \\ \hline 12 \\ 12 \\ \hline \end{array}$$

16. 4 x 25 x 5.2 = 520
17. 52 + 45 = 97
18. 15 x (50 + 3) = 750 + 45 = 795
19. 600 + 13 = 613
20. $\frac{21}{4} - \frac{5}{2} = \frac{21}{4} - \frac{10}{4} = \frac{11}{4} = 2\frac{3}{4}$
21. $\frac{14}{30} - \frac{5}{30} = \frac{9}{30} = \frac{3}{10}$
22. $\frac{13}{4} + \frac{15}{8} = \frac{26}{8} + \frac{15}{8} = \frac{41}{8} = 5\frac{1}{8}$
23. 0.123
24. $\frac{3}{4} = \frac{3 \times 25}{4 \times 25} = \frac{75}{100} = 75\%$
25. $1\frac{3}{4} = 1\frac{9}{12}$; $1\frac{2}{3} = 1\frac{8}{12}$; $1\frac{3}{4}$ is bigger.
26. 21 = 3 x 7 ; 35 = 5 x 7 ; G.C.F. of 21 and 35 = 7
27. 25 = 5 x 5 ; 40 = 2 x 2 x 2 x 5 ;
    L.C.M. of 25 and 40 = 2 x 2 x 2 x 5 x 5 = 200
28. A = 07:00   B = 22:00   C = 08:30   D = 23:30
29. 15 hours
30. 15 hours
31. 6.2 m/s
32. 133 s
33. 240 s
34. She should go to Lucy's convenience store because Ben's convenience store will be closed as she needs 133 s to go there.
35. Amount : 15 x 20 + 12 x 5 = 360 ; She has $360 in all.
36. Amount in $20 : 15 x 20 = 300
    Fraction : $\frac{300}{360} = \frac{5}{6}$
    $\frac{5}{6}$ of Mrs. Saura's money is in $20 bill.
37. $\frac{1}{3}$
38. $\frac{2}{15}$
39. 33.33%
40. 20%
41. 1 : 5
42. 69 popsicles
43. $29.95
44. $0.45
45. 3 packs
46. $33.92
47. $15
48. 200 slices

8 Perimeter and Area

1. 8 ; 12 ; 11 ; 20 ; 20 ; 32
2. 4 ; 8 ; 7 ; 25 ; 21 ; 64
3. P : (7 + 6) x 2 ; 26   A : 7 x 5 ; 35
4. P : (12 + 10) x 2 ; 44   A : 12 x 9 ; 108
5. P : (60 + 25) x 2 ; 170   A : 60 x 20 ; 1200
6. P : (18 + 3.5) x 2 ; 43   A : 18 x 3 ; 54

7. P : 8 + 11 + 12 ; 31   A : 12 x 7 ÷ 2 ; 42
8. P : 13 + 5 + 12 ; 30   A : 12 x 5 ÷ 2 ; 30
9. P : 16 + 10 + 10 ; 36   A : 16 x 6 ÷ 2 ; 48
10. P : 6.4 + 4.5 + 3 ; 13.9   A : 3 x 4 ÷ 2 ; 6
11.-15. (Suggested answers)
11.
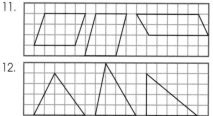
12.
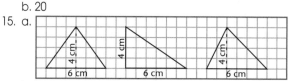
13.
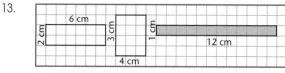
b. 26
14. a.
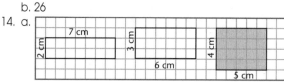
b. 20
15. a.

b. the same   c. different   d. the same
16. a. Fencing needed : 8.5 x 2 + 6 x 2 = 17 + 12 = 29 ;
    29 m of fencing are needed to enclose the field.
    b. Turf needed : 8.5 x 6 = 51 ;
    51 m² of turf must be laid to cover the whole field.
17. No. of times : (27 x 21) ÷ (9 x 7) = 9 ;
    The poster is 9 times bigger than the card.
18. a. Area of the door : 2 x 1.2 = 2.4 ;
    Area of the door is 2.4 m².
    b. Total area of the wall and the door : 5 x 2.4 = 12 ;
    Area of the wall : 12 – 2.4 = 9.6 ;
    Area of the wall is 9.6 m².
19. Area enclosed : 13 x 20 ÷ 2 = 130 ;
    Area enclosed is 130 km².

Mind Boggler

21 m²

9 Volume and Mass

1. 750 cm³
2. 78 m³
3. 9.6 m³
4. 1 km³
5. 24 cm³
6. 60 cm³
7. 4913 cm³
8. 28 km³
9. 384 cm²
10. 1536 cm³
11. 30 720 cm³
12. Yes. Thickness of each book is 4 cm, so the total thickness of 20 books is 80 cm or 0.8 m.
13. B
14. 84 blocks
15. 24 blocks
16. 19 ; 6 ; 25 ; 2850 cm³
17. 12 ; 12 ; 12 ; 1728 cm³
18. 12 ; 6 ; 6 ; 432 cm³
19. 5 ; 6 ; 21 ; 630 cm³
20. 22 ; 5 ; 3 ; 330 cm³
21. 15 ; 4 ; 23 ; 1380 cm³
22. E; C; D; F; B; A
23. 1000
24. 37.5
25. 7
26. 20
27. 111 cm³
28. 96 cm³
29. 81 cm³
30. Amount of water : 60 x 30 x 15 ÷ 1000 = 27 ;
    It contains 27 litres of water.

31. Increase in depth : 16 – 15 = 1 cm ;
    Increase in volume of water : 60 x 30 x 1 = 1800 cm³
    = 1800 mL ; 1.8 L of water must be added.
32. Volume of water : 18 L = 18 000 mL ;
    Base area of the pool : 60 x 30 = 1800 cm² ;
    Depth of the water : 10 cm ;
    Depth of water in the pool is 10 cm.
33. Capacity : 60 x 30 x 25 = 45 000 mL ;
    Capacity of the pool is 45 L.
34. 290 g   35. 350 g
36. 110 g   37. 81 g
38. 11.6 kg   39. 4.05 kg
40. 3 tablets   41. 1 g

Mind Boggler

1. 0.25 g   2. 7.75 g

10 Symmetry, 2-D and 3-D Figures

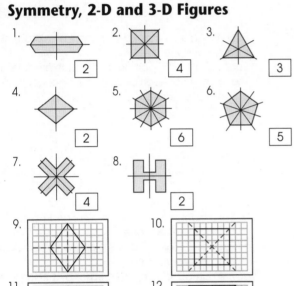

1. 2   2. 4   3. 3
4. 2   5. 6   6. 5
7. 4   8. 2

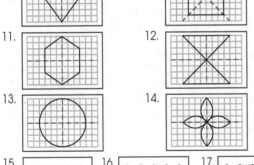

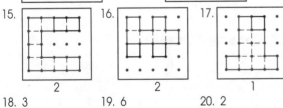

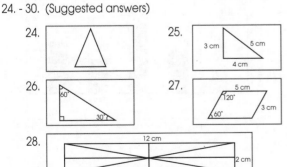

9. 10. 11. 12. 13. 14.
15. 2   16. 2   17. 1
18. 3   19. 6   20. 2
21. 2   22. 2   23. 4
24. - 30. (Suggested answers)

24.
25. 3 cm 5 cm 4 cm
26. 60° 30°
27. 5 cm 120° 60° 3 cm
28. 12 cm 2 cm

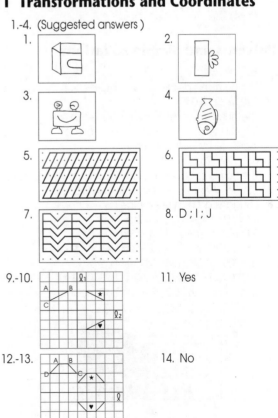

29.   30.
31. ④   32. ⑤
33. ⑤   34. ⑧
35.   36.   37.

38. A : square ; B : rhombus ; C : trapezoid ;
    D : parallelogram ; E : kite ; F : rectangle
39. Rectangle ; Rhombus ; Parallelogram ; Square
40. Rhombus ; Square   41. Rectangle; Parallelogram
42. Rectangle ; Square   43. Rhombus ; Parallelogram
44. Cube   45. Tetrahedron
46. Rectangular pyramid or Triangular prism
47. Square

Mind Boggler

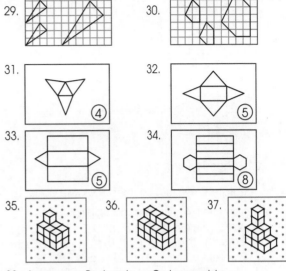

11 Transformations and Coordinates

1.-4. (Suggested answers)

1.   2.
3.   4.
5.   6.
7.   8. D ; I ; J

9.-10.   11. Yes

12.-13.   14. No

15.-16.   17. No

18.-19.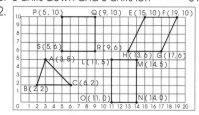

20. (Suggested answer)

    Rotate ♥ $\frac{1}{4}$ turn counter clockwise about 0. Then translate it 4 units up and 2 units right.

21. A (2 , 6) ; B (6 , 1) ; C (12 , 0) ; D (0 , 3) ; E (5 , 6) ;
    F (5 , 12) ; G (8 , 12) ; H (3 , 0) ; I (1 , 12) ; J (0 , 10)

22. Parallelogram   23. E and F
24. I, F and G   25. H and C
26. D and J   27. 9 square units
28. 7 square units   29. (7 , 9)
30. 6 units down and 3 units left   31. 9 units right

32.

33. Its ordered pair will be (4 , 6), ABC is an isosceles triangle.
34. Its ordered pair will be (15 , 6), EFGH is a trapezoid.

Mind Boggler

(3 , 4)

12 Patterns and Simple Equations

1. 80 ; 70 ; 58 ;
   The numbers decrease by 2 more each time.
2. 120 ; 720 ; 5 040 ;
   The numbers multiply by 1 more each time.
3. 52 ; 50 ; 53 ; The numbers decrease by 2 and then increase by 1 alternatively.
4. 65 ; 129 ; 257 ;
   The numbers double the previous number and minus 1.
5. 25 ; 36 ; 49 ; The numbers are 1x1, 2x2, 3x3, ...
6.-8. (Suggested answers for the number pairs)
6. 6 ; 4 ; 9 ; 1st + 2nd – 1 = 3rd
7. 24 ; 6 ; 5 ; 1st ÷ 2nd + 1 = 3rd
8. 6 ; 8 ; 22 ; 1st + 2nd x 2 = 3rd
9. a. 2000 ; 2005 ; 125 ; 149   b. 2 010
10. a. 1999 ; 2000 ; 9.00 ; 9.50   b. $10.50
11. a. 4 ; 5 ; 6 ; 4.6 ; 5.2 ; 5.9   b. 7 months
12. a.

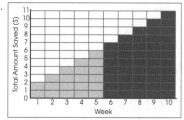

b. $13   c. Week 19
d. His savings increase by $1 more each week.

13. a.
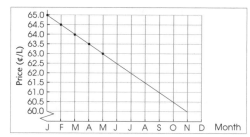

b. 62.5¢ per litre   c. November

14. a.
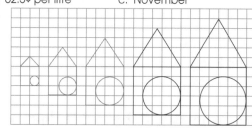

b. Each triangle is 1 block wider and 1 block taller than the previous one.
c. Each square is 1 block longer than the previous one.
d. The diameter of each circle is 1 block longer than the previous one.

15. a.
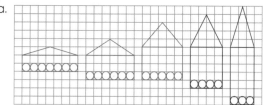

b. Each triangle is 1 block narrower and 1 block taller than the previous one.
c. Each rectangle is 1 block shorter and 1 block taller than the previous one.
d. The number of circle decreases by 1 each time.

16. 28   17. 100   18. 28
19. 15   20. 22   21. 88
22. 115   23. 147   24. 4
25. 9   26. 5   27. 96
28. 15   29. 20   30. 6
31. 7   32. 26   33. 7

Mind Boggler

13 ; 16 ; 19 ; 21 ; 24 ; 30

13 Data and Graphs

1. L   2. B   3. C   4. B
5. L   6. C   7. B   8. L
9. B   10. B

11. a. 5 ; 8 ; 4 ; 6 ;   b. $\frac{5}{30}$; $\frac{8}{30}$; $\frac{4}{30}$; $\frac{6}{30}$

12.
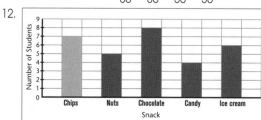

13.

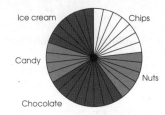

8. Misty, Sunny, Rainy, Cloudy

9.

X	1	2	3	4
1	1	2	3	4
2	2	4	6	8
3	3	6	9	12
4	4	8	12	16

10. 16

14. a. 60.1¢/L   b. 59.2 ¢/L   c. 56.9 ¢/L

15. a. 2.9   b. 2.5   c. 2   16. a. 18   b. 15   c. 15

17. a. 50%, 50%, 50%, 60%, 60%, 80%, 80%, 80%, 80%, 80%
b. 67%   c. 70%   d. 80%

18. $\frac{9}{36}$ 19. $\frac{16}{36}$ 20. $\frac{27}{36}$

11. 4   12. $\frac{3}{16}$ 13. 3

14. $\frac{3}{16}$ 15. $\frac{4}{16}$ or $\frac{1}{4}$

21. a.

No. of Minutes	Tally	No. of Students
1 - 20	|||	3
21 - 40	|||||	5
41 - 60	|||	3
61 - 80	|||	3
81 -100			1

b.

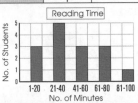

c. 4 students

16.

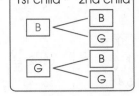

17. 4 ; BB, BG, GB and GG

18. $\frac{1}{4}$ 19. $\frac{2}{4}$ or $\frac{1}{2}$

22. a.

No. of Hours	Tally	No. of Students
1 - 2	|||	3
3 - 4			1
5 - 6	||||	4
7 - 8	|||	3
9 - 10	||||	4

b.

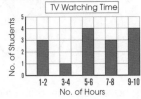

c. 7 students

20.

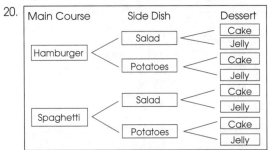

21. 8   22. 4   23. 4

24. 2   25. $\frac{1}{8}$ 26. $\frac{1}{8}$

27. They are S & Co, S & T, H & Co, H & T, D & Co, D & T, M & Co, M & T, C & Co and C & T.

28. $\frac{1}{10}$

29.

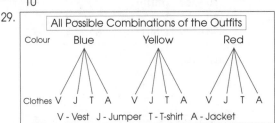

Mind Boggler

(Suggested answer) 4, 8 and 18

14 Probability

1. a. $\frac{5}{20}$ or $\frac{1}{4}$ b. $\frac{6}{20}$ or $\frac{3}{10}$ c. $\frac{4}{20}$ or $\frac{1}{5}$
d. $\frac{2}{20}$ or $\frac{1}{10}$ e. $\frac{3}{20}$ f. $\frac{9}{20}$

2.

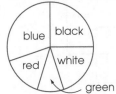

3. (Suggested answer)
Put more red marbles into the box.

4. Cloudy   5. Rainy   6. $\frac{7}{10}$

7. $\frac{1}{6}$, $\frac{1}{5}$, $\frac{3}{10}$, $\frac{1}{3}$

30. $\frac{1}{12}$ 31. $\frac{4}{12}$ or $\frac{1}{3}$ 32. $\frac{3}{12}$ or $\frac{1}{4}$

33. a. 9   b. Jacket   c. $\frac{1}{12}$
d. $\frac{2}{12}$ or $\frac{1}{6}$ e. $\frac{2}{12}$ or $\frac{1}{6}$

Mind Boggler

$\frac{2}{6}$ or $\frac{1}{3}$

Final Test

1. A	2. D	3. A
4. C	5. A	6. C
7. B	8. C	9. C
10. D	11. A	12. B

13. A
14. C
15. B
16. C
17. A
18. C
19. C
20. B
21. D
22. C
23. B
24. B
25. C
26. B
27. 3.249
28. 9.84
29. 17.946
30. 108.3
31. 108
32. 164
33. 20
34. 211
35. 5 ; 75
36. 4 ; 49
37. 18 ; 25
38. 16 ; 2 ; 32
39. a. 2 x 3 x 3 ; 2 x 2 x 2 x 3   b. 6 ; 72
40. a. 2 x 2 x 3 x 3 ; 2 x 2 x 11   b. 4 ; 396
41. $1\frac{5}{12}$
42. $\frac{1}{8}$
43. $\frac{7}{20}$
44. $\frac{13}{24}$
45. $\frac{3}{8}$
46. $\frac{1}{12}$
47. $\frac{1}{2}$
48. $\frac{1}{10}$
49. $\frac{7}{8}$
50. $\frac{9}{20}$
51. $1\frac{2}{9}$
52. $2\frac{19}{30}$
53. 3300 cm³
54. 5.4 m³
55. 4875 cm³
56. B

57.
58.
59.

4   4   1

60. 129 , 257 , 513; Time 2, minus 1.
61. 50, 35, 27.5; Divide by 2, plus 10.
62. 2
63. 27
64. 12.5
65. 5.3
66. 262.5
67. 56
68. Steve
69. Fred
70. $2\frac{11}{12}$
71. $1\frac{1}{12}$
72. $1.08
73. 11.25 kg
74. 40
75. 80
76. 18
77. 12
78. 14

79.
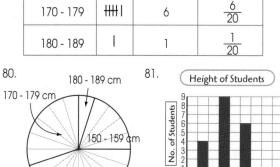

Range of Height (cm)	Tally	No. of Students	Fraction of the Whole
150 - 159	IIII	4	$\frac{4}{20}$
160 - 169	HHH IIII	9	$\frac{9}{20}$
170 - 179	HHH I	6	$\frac{6}{20}$
180 - 189	I	1	$\frac{1}{20}$

80.
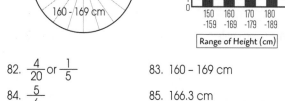

81.
Height of Students

82. $\frac{4}{20}$ or $\frac{1}{5}$
83. 160 – 169 cm
84. $\frac{5}{6}$
85. 166.3 cm

Game Cards

A. 1. Fill up the 3-L container with water and empty it into the 5-L container.
   2. Fill up the 3-L container again and pour the water to fill up the 5-L container. 1 L of water is left in the 3-L container.
   3. Empty the 5-L container.
   4. Pour the 1 L of water from the 3-L container into the 5-L container.
   5. Fill up the 3-L container again and empty it into the 5-L container. There are exactly 4 L of water in the 5-L container.

B. a. Either Sean or Ray likes hockey. Teddy and Bill don't like hockey.
   b. Either Teddy or Ray likes basketball. Sean and Bill don't like basketball.
   c. Bill's brother likes soccer. Bill doesn't like soccer. From a, b, and c, you know that Bill likes baseball. From the clues d, you know that Teddy doesn't like basketball. Therefore Ray likes basketball, Sean likes hockey, and Teddy likes soccer.

C. (Suggested answers)

1	3	6
2	5	7
4	8	9

1	4	6
2	5	8
3	7	9

1	2	5
3	4	6
7	8	9

1	3	4
2	6	7
5	8	9

1	2	4
3	5	6
7	8	9

1	3	5
2	4	6
7	8	9

D. (Suggested answers)

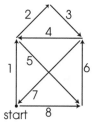
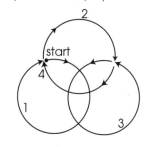

E. If all the animals have 4 legs, the total number of legs is 25 x 4 = 100.
   Number of extra legs = 100 – 70 = 30
   Number of chickens = 30 ÷ 2 = 15
   Number of dogs and cows = 25 – 15 = 10
Since there are 4 more dogs than cows,
   Number of cows = (10 – 4) ÷ 2 = 6 ÷ 2 = 3
   Number of dogs = 3 + 4 = 7
There are 7 dogs, 3 cows and 15 chickens.

F.
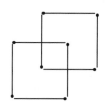

8 matches can form 2 large squares and 1 small square.